Break-Away Thinking

Break-Away Thinking

How to Challenge Your
Business Assumptions
(and Why You Should)

Ian I. Mitroff
Harold Quinton Distinguished Professor
of Business Policy and
Co-director, Center for Crisis Management
University of Southern California

WILEY

JOHN WILEY & SONS
New York   Chichester   Brisbane   Toronto   Singapore

ISBN 0-471-60202-7

Printed in the United States of America

10 9 8 7 6 5 4 3 2 1

To my daughter, Dana

The problems of life are insoluble on the surface.

Ludwig Wittgenstein

Imagination is more important than knowledge.

Albert Einstein

Seek greater understanding, but do not expect greater detail. There are many who, by virtue of their passivity, dependency, fear and laziness, seek to be shown every inch of the way and have it demonstrated to them that each step will be safe and worth their while. This cannot be done. For the journey of spiritual growth requires courage and initiative and independence of thought and action. While the words of the prophets and the assistance of grace are available, the journey must still be traveled alone. No teacher can carry you there. There are no preset formulas. Rituals are only learning aids, they are not the learning.

M. Scott Peck
The Road Less Traveled
pp. 310-313

Acknowledgments

The tables in Memo 7 first appeared in *Business Not As Usual* and are reprinted by permission of Jossey-Bass Inc. Publishers; portions of Memos 11, 12, and 13 first appeared in an article in the *Sloan Management Review* and are reprinted by permission.

Contents

xi

Contents

Prologue

I

The basic argument of this book is as follows:

1. On every front of our existence, the problems the United States faces today cannot even be properly defined, let alone solved, in terms of the old prevailing solutions. In short, the old solutions just don't work anymore.

2. The old solutions are the product of old ways of thinking.

3. We require bold, radically new ways of thinking if we are to obtain the new solutions necessary to meet our problems.

4. The new thinking we require cannot result unless we first understand the deeper patterns or road maps of reality that lie beneath the old ways of thinking.

5. Change, like life itself, is difficult and often painful. There is no hope of attaining new ways of thinking unless there is a full and honest acceptance of both the pain and the joy involved if human beings are to grow.

6. The pain and joy of life cannot be discussed or written about in dry, academic prose because such language fails to do justice to the depth of our emotions. Indeed, not only does it seriously distort their nature but it renders the experience of them meaningless.

7. Thus, the new solutions cannot be expressed in terms of our old familiar concepts or lan-

guage; they must be expressed with a new vocabulary—a new language, as it were, for thinking new thoughts.

One of the great paradoxes of life is that the more we resist the notion that change, like life itself, is difficult and often painful, the more painful we make it. The other side of the paradox is that the more we accept the notion that life is difficult and often painful, the less painful and even the more joyful it becomes. To seek the joy of living we must be prepared to accept its pain.

II

This book is about mental road maps and the need to change them if we are to tame the problems facing us. It is also about the joy that comes from using the human capacity for reason to think through difficult challenges.

Fundamentally, this is a book about the mental pictures we all carry around in our heads to make sense of the world. It is about how to function when the familiar maps that we have depended on for so long to guide our behavior no longer work, indeed mislead us seriously if we persist in following them.

The notion of a "mental road map" is more than just a convenient metaphor. The concept of maps is deeply ingrained in the human mind. Maps are used not only to show the locations of things, places, and ideas in relation to one another, but even more important, to give us a sense of the "lay of the land" or "the big picture"—where things fit or lie in relation to everything else.

Maps no longer work when the world they are supposed to describe changes abruptly. The most radical break occurs when not only relative placement and distances between objects but the very *names* of the objects are changed; the overall effect is that the entire landscape has been altered drastically. When this occurs we experience extreme discomfort and severe disorientation. Nothing fits, nothing works anymore. We are lost, adrift, in the most profound sense of the term. Indeed, if the alteration of our maps becomes so severe that we can no longer function at all, we speak literally of a "break with reality."

Break-Away Thinking is concerned with explaining and understanding the fundamental changes that have occurred in the structure of the world since World War II. It is concerned with the new thinking required to make sense of and to function within the new highly interdependent, highly coupled, global economy and society that have arisen since World War II, coming to the fore especially in the last five to ten years.

The basic argument of *Break-Away Thinking* is that we cannot understand, and certainly cannot function within, the new global economy using the old maps of reality that were appropriate for the world prior to World War II. The old maps are by now so seriously out of touch with reality that they threaten economic ruin for those who persist in following them.

The net effect of the global economy is that *everything* is not only interconnected but also potentially capable of affecting everything else. As a result, *events everywhere have now become local news.* In case there is any doubt, one need only mention Bhopal and Chernobyl. The effect is a world far more complex and chaotic than anything our ancestors ever envisioned or had to face. As a consequence, the rules of doing business have changed so radically that entirely new ways of thinking are needed if businesses, let alone nations as a whole, are to survive in today's environment.

It has become a cliché to argue that the problems we face now are so serious that they require bold, new solutions to make headway in solving them. It has also become something of a cliché to argue that these new solutions can only be obtained if we are prepared to develop entirely new ways of thinking. Clichés or not, new solutions and new ways of thinking are absolutely necessary. New thinking can be practiced only if we have a basic understanding of why the global economy follows a set of rules so different from anything we've ever encountered before that in effect we need an entirely different concept of the world if we are to function at all. *Break-Away*

Thinking is concerned not only with these new sets of rules but also with the larger road map or concept of reality within which these rules function, and indeed, from which the rules derive in the first place.

III

Break-Away Thinking aims to get to the heart of a relatively small number of vital issues with which top executives in all businesses must deal repeatedly. These issues are critical not only because they affect top executives and their corporations but because they affect us all. They affect the economic health of our entire society, and thereby our personal economic health; they affect our social well-being, or quality of life, as well. For this reason alone, *Break-Away Thinking* deals with issues of importance to all citizens.

We are caught between overwhelming complexity on the one hand and almost insurmountable pressures on the other to treat all complex issues simplistically. What can we do to steer an intelligent course between these twin destroyers of our ability to make sense of a world seemingly gone berserk? This book penetrates to the heart of key issues by examining them through a series of memos written between fictionalized chief executive officers (CEOs) of fictionalized major corporations. Although the names of the characters and their corporations are fabricated, the issues with which they are struggling are not. Indeed, the content of the memos and the style in which they are written come directly from my own research and consulting experience in working with major corporations and government agencies over many years.

The point of the book is certainly *not* how to write better memos. In this sense, it is anything but another of the trivial "how-to" books that have flooded the business sections of most large bookstores. The purpose of using memos is to effect a different style of language in order to convey critical ideas succinctly.

Even though it was certainly not primarily or even intentionally written for professional philosophers, *Break-Away Thinking* is a frank philosophical book. Indeed, as I write these words, a professor of business from one of Japan's leading universities has just completed a visit with me. Every one of our many conversations emphasized repeatedly that the Japanese and Americans *organize* their business and industrial systems differently because they *think* differently about the world. They have fundamentally differing mental pictures about the nature of the world. To make no bones about it, there is more than just an economic competition occurring between our two countries. Fundamentally, it is a philosophical competition over the nature of man, work, organizations, and even culture.

We are not obliged to think like the Japanese and certainly not to be like them. But we are obliged to learn to shift our thinking if that is what the world now demands of us. At a minimum, we must understand *why* the world requires a different mode of thinking. Whether we want to and have the will to shift is another matter.

There is evidence from a recent book by the pollster Lou Harris that the American public is beginning to understand, at least at an intuitive level, that serious and deep changes are required in the ways we think about problems—if not the world itself—in order to come up with the radical and creative solutions we need. I quote:

> The impact of the reality of [increased foreign] competition has been to convince a solid 59%-38% majority that wages should go up only as productivity increases. The appeal of unions that they can get better wages appears to have been undermined by this greater realization. Thus, it seems logical that unions had better begin thinking in terms of productivity as much as they do about wages. Such approaches would appear to make more sense than relying on raising import barriers and even tariffs to keep out foreign competition. In the long term, American labor must face the challenge of how to educate and train a labor force that is much more proficient in science, math, technology, that is capable of thinking problems through, is able to find answers to questions they do not know the answers to, and is so creative and well trained that they would be the basis for a whole new economy that would out compete any other economy on the face of the earth. This would mean new industries with new types of work configurations, and new standards of productivity re-

flective of much higher worker capabilities. When just such a scenario was recently described to a cross section of the public, a four-to-one majority said it made sense to them. (Louis Harris, *Inside America*. New York: Vintage Books, Random House, 1987, p. 221)

What's needed is to take the next step, that is, to move beyond intuition to a deeper understanding of the new ways in which we must think.

Let's take a look, then, at a series of exchanges between two CEOs struggling to deal with the issues that perplex them, that they are paid handsomely to deal with, and that they have chosen the challenge of dealing with.

MEMOS 1 & 2

*Quality Doesn't Stop
at the Factory Walls*

TO: Robert Fountain, CEO and President
Fountain Industries

FROM: Steven Hart, CEO and President
Hart Industries

DATE: May 11, 1988

SUBJECT: Manufacturing Quality! If We Don't
Get It Soon We're in Deep Trouble

Bob, I want to reiterate how good it was to meet
you and to talk with you at the CEOs' forum the
other day. I got so many good ideas, the whole
thing was so stimulating, that my head is still
reeling. I think what really struck me was that
for all the differences between our businesses,
the products we produce and sell, there is an
amazing amount of similarity in our problems.

Of all the people I met and heard the other
day, you really stood out! You have a way of
grasping ideas, issues, and problems and of pen-
etrating to their heart that really impressed me.

Excuse my writing to you in the form of a
memo, but it comes easiest to me. I want to take
you up on your kind offer to continue the dialogue between us. I think in the beginning you
can do more for me than I can for you, but I hope
I can return the favor shortly.

Frankly, I sense we could really help one another. Let me get right to the point. I have always

been more comfortable with ideas than with people. Indeed, I like to believe that I've been blessed with a talent for seeing the big picture, for seeing around corners, for intuiting the new directions in which the world is headed long before others can see them.

I sense that while you share with me an intense interest in ideas as well, and the ability to see the big picture, your particular strength lies in dealing with people. I don't have to be convinced that people are important and that you can't treat them as machines. I've never believed that you can. However, I just don't have as good an intuitive sense when it comes to dealing with people as I do when dealing with more abstract issues such as what new businesses make sense for today's environment.

I feel lately that problems are coming at me from all sides. It seems that I just begin to recognize the existence of a problem, let alone grapple with it, when another one, even more grotesque and horrendous, bears down on me. I feel as if I'm being buried alive in a swamp or a blizzard of overwhelming problems. I can't even begin to list them.

Let me start with one, however, that seems to be at the heart of many of the problems we face. Quality!

We've never really been at the top of our industry in producing high-quality products. Don't get me wrong. We've never produced shoddy items, let alone knowingly sold hazardous or defective products. It's just that quality has never seemed to make it to the top of our priority list. If anything, I guess I'm as guilty as the next guy of saying that meeting our production quotas is our number one priority.

It's not that we haven't tried to upgrade our quality. It's worse than that. Everything we've tried has backfired. We tried establishing tough quotas. We wrote and distributed strict manufacturing guidelines, but no one took them seriously. Frankly, I'm not only stymied, I'm at my wit's end. As you know, the new global competition is so tough out there that if we don't start producing products that are substantially higher in quality than anything we've been able to manufacture thus far, I don't think we'll be able to stay in business.

I need your thoughts. I don't expect or even want them to be specific, since you'd have to know our business to do that. Rather, I want to learn from your *general* experience. What are your *general* thoughts?

TO: Steve Hart
Hart Industries

FROM: Bob Fountain
Fountain Industries

DATE: May 13, 1988

SUBJECT: Quality Isn't Just the Name of the
Game; It is *The Whole* Game!

Steve, don't apologize for the memo format. I use
it all the time. Also, don't apologize for calling on
me. I'm glad to respond—it gives me the opportunity to put my ideas into a coherent form. Indeed, I'd like to do it since sometimes I believe
I'm more of a writer and a thinker than I am a
CEO of an equipment manufacturing company.

Steve, you're right. Even though I love ideas,
I'm basically more at home with people. Maybe a
better way to put it is that I especially love those
ideas that relate directly to people.

Let me lay out two contrasting sets of assumptions or belief systems side by side. The left-hand
set of assumptions represents what we used to
believe (and what many organizations still do believe) about how to obtain quality. The right-hand
side represents what we painfully discovered
through trial and error before, thank God, we almost went out of business. As you can see, both
sets relate directly to what people believe about

16

what motivates workers, how to run an organization, how to set priorities, and so forth.

Of course your situation is complicated by
specifics I can't possibly know. But even so, I
believe the primary task of leadership is to rise
above such specifics and get to the core of the
issue. The core is *always* represented by a set of
assumptions we carry around in our heads about
how the world is supposed to function. When the
world doesn't work that way, we crash because
of the inappropriateness of our beliefs. The only
specifics, the only details, that matter from this
perspective are those that give us a valid reading
on the reasonableness of those assumptions. In
any case, let me lay out the assumptions. I hope
they reveal that, like you, I initially defined the
problem of achieving quality too narrowly. As
a result, I got trapped into *solving the wrong
problem too precisely.*

Quality cannot be ob-tained with the following beliefs; hence they are	Quality can potentially be obtained with these beliefs; hence they are
Inappropriate Assumptions.	*Appropriate Assumptions.*
1. Quality can be achieved without a deeply internalized need and concern for its attainment and what it's all about on the	**1.** Quality cannot be achieved without a deeply internalized need and concern for it on the part of everyone connected with the

part of workers and even supervisors and managers; i.e., it can come down from "on high" through rules and procedures.

organization at every level of its operation.

2a. Quality can be achieved only by setting explicit goals and targets that establish tight controls over the production process.

2a. Quality demands workers, supervisors, and managers who exhibit a clear and persistent demand for its attainment and who will strive for its constant improvement even when lacking explicit goals to guide them.

b. Conversely, to achieve quality, it is enough (sufficient) to set explicit goals and targets.

b. Both explicit goals and targets in the form of a consistent set of policies and attitudes that are widely shared throughout the organization and an implicit desire on the part of everyone to go beyond written policies are necessary to achieve quality.

c. It is enough to have written policies that, once communicated, can sit on a shelf.

c. A single, unequivocal message must be communicated repeatedly and persistently that product quality is a goal that all members of the organization should share and strive to achieve.

3a. Quality can be achieved even though meeting production schedules, i.e., getting products out the door, is the number one goal of the organization.

3a. Quality can only be achieved by making it the number one goal of the organization, which no other goals must be allowed to dominate.

b. Quality can be achieved as a secondary or even a tertiary goal.

b. Managers must emphasize that quality is their primary manufacturing objective.

c. Making a profit is the ultimate goal that must dominate all other goals of the organization.

c. One must not only understand but believe firmly and deeply that one will not make profits unless the desire to make money is subordinated to the love of making quality goods; one must love being in the business one is in; one must enjoy making one's products for their own sake.

4. Workers aren't concerned about quality or at best have a relatively low interest in it.

4. There are workers who have a primary interest in making quality products or who can develop such an interest; you must make it a top priority to hire only these kinds of workers.

5a. Factories are essentially closed systems.

5a. Factories are essentially open systems.

b. Therefore, the achievement of quality is mainly accomplished inside the walls of the factory, i.e., by considering only those factors that are internal to the organization.

b. Therefore, the achievement of quality is accomplished by considering factors both inside and outside the walls of the factory; both must be given equal weight in the design and running of the organization.

c. Therefore, the causes of poor qual-

c. Therefore, the causes of poor quality are traceable mainly to a poor workforce, poor workmanship, and poor maintenance of production facilities and equipment.

ity may be due not only to a poor workforce, etc., but also to such factors as poor incoming parts, materials, or even the basic design of products.

d. Therefore, blame for poor quality can be traced immediately to internal causes.

d. Therefore, blame must be traced to its ultimate sources whether they are inside or outside the walls of the organization, or both.

e. Therefore, workers are the most obvious candidates for blame.

e. Therefore, workers become scapegoats when problems are not traced back through the production chain to their "true" source.

The bottom line is that you can't get quality through blame or through fixing the wrong part of the whole system.

Send more problems so we can bat some more ideas back and forth. I love a good game of intellectual Ping-Pong!

To Remove a Problem—To Change a System—You May Have to Make It Worse Before It Can Get Better

TO: Bob Fountain
          Fountain Industries

FROM: Steve Hart
          Hart Industries

DATE: May 20, 1988

SUBJECT: Now That I Understand the Problem,
              How the Hell Do I Make It Better?

You're on! I love Ping-Pong, too, especially when it involves batting ideas back and forth.

If I truly understand your previous memo, we've been as guilty as anybody of proceeding on the wrong assumptions on how to obtain quality. I have no doubt that we need to change our assumptions and, if I understand you, develop new policies and procedures, based on a different set of beliefs. Unless we change our basic ways of thinking about the problem, we'll just keep recreating it in different forms in various parts of our organization.

However, I now have a new problem that may be even worse than the first one. How the hell do I change the old assumptions in our organization that locked us into *not* obtaining quality? Who owns those assumptions? What buttons, what levers do I push to change them? What do I do, hold a big meeting and say here's what we now need to believe in? Should I issue a set of internal memos saying that by next Monday or Tuesday we will ditch the wrong set of assumptions and adopt the right ones? Again, I'm not looking for specifics, but a general way out of the forest. Any advice you have would be most welcome.

TO: Steve Hart
Hart Industries

FROM: Bob Fountain
Fountain Industries

DATE: May 25, 1988

SUBJECT: The Paradox of Massive Change!

I assure you that it's only because we made the
very same wrong assumptions about people
that you did, for so long, that we finally learned
through painful experience that if we didn't
change, we'd perish. Now I'm going to be absolutely straight with you, because if we're going
to play Ping-Pong and get something out of it,
there's no other way to play.

You say that I have a talent for dealing with
people. Well if I do, it didn't fall from the heavens.
It's not just a random gift from the gods. Rather,
it's a result of my finally going back to school
and studying formally what makes people tick.
I always had an interest in psychology. The kind
of problems we were facing pushed me over the
edge and forced me to do some systematic study.
If I hadn't been studying psychology, I doubt that
what I and our organization finally did would
have been sufficient to get us out of the same
kind of mess that you find yourself in. But let me

back up and give you some thoughts in what I hope is a logical order.

How does an individual, let alone a whole organization, change? That's one of the thorniest problems around. Again, there are too many specifics involved for me to know which particular levers to push in your organization, but let me give you two ways of thinking about the whole process of change that I've found to be immensely helpful.

First, before I even begin, you've got to realize that, like us, you may not be able to achieve the change you desire without the help of a specially trained organizational change agent, preferably somebody who knows a lot about family therapy. The reason is that there are just too many powerful, complex forces going on in organizations, many of which we're only barely aware of. And without such knowledge, you can easily destroy the whole system.

The first, basic question you or the person you bring in to help you has to ask is: Are the problems our organization is facing basically explicit, on the surface, rational, and thus amenable to fairly direct strategies of change? For example, let's say that your biggest problem is to change your organization's image of itself from that of a "closed system" to that of an "open system." In order to do this, do you merely have to give your people instruction in understanding complex systems? Or do you have to hire new people who can understand this from the very beginning? Do you have to change your entire reward system as well, so that people will be rewarded explicitly for the new behaviors you want from them? Do you have to change the power structure, the number of layers and levels in the system that people report to? Do you have to change your whole organizational communication pattern? For instance, do you have to redesign the memos, worksheets, and even order forms that pass back and forth not only within the factory but outside as well, say to your suppliers, so that you can see that *they* are also part of the whole system and make them an explicit part of it? So the second question you've got to ask yourself is: Can I accomplish what I need to by simply asking these kinds of questions?

Let me quickly outline a method of managing change that I've found very helpful over the years. Look at the diagram on the next page.

Take a look not only at the dimensions of the figure but also at the cells and what they mean. In undertaking any change program, I differentiate between things that need to be kept the same or preserved and those that absolutely need to change if the organization or system is going to function in today's complex environment. I use the diagram explicitly to place various factors or things that need to be assessed and to see how they fall.

Look at Cell 1. I hope it's clear that this cell

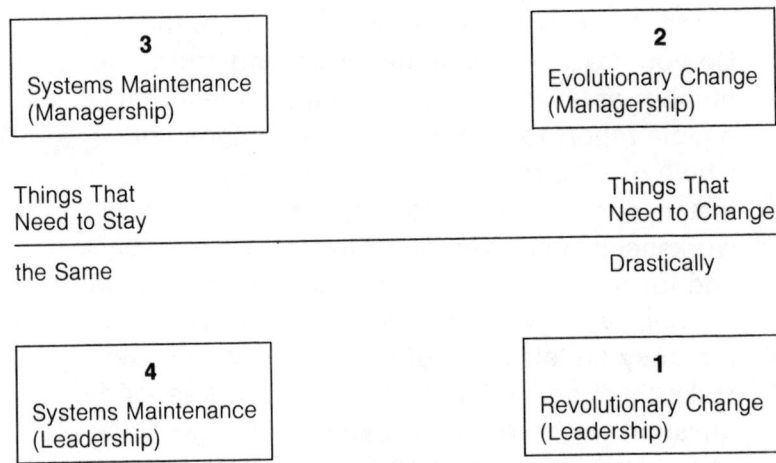

**Things That Are
Easy to Change**

| **3**
Systems Maintenance
(Managership) | | **2**
Evolutionary Change
(Managership) |

Things That
Need to Stay

Things That
Need to Change

the Same

Drastically

| **4**
Systems Maintenance
(Leadership) | | **1**
Revolutionary Change
(Leadership) |

**Things That Are
Difficult to Change**

calls for extreme leadership. By definition, you've got to make a lot of changes, and you and/or the other key players in your organization judge that the changes will be difficult to make. For example, go back to the assumptions in our last memo. A difficult change for your organization may be to move from blaming workers and internal factors for the production of poor-quality items to seeing that poor quality can be attributed to any part of a complex system.

So Cell 1 calls for leadership because you're talking about revolutionary change. You're talking

30

about really shocking and jolting the system out of its doldrums.

Now take a look at Cell 2. I hope it's obvious that this is really "managership," not leadership, because you're talking about evolutionary change, change that the system can accomplish almost by itself, without any serious disruption. You can almost orchestrate such change as a programmed series of instructions, that is, "change by the numbers." The same holds for Cell 3. Cell 4 again calls for leadership because you're talking about preserving sacred and cherished values of the organization that you don't want to change— for example, good esprit de corps, treating people with respect, and so forth.

The point is that you can use this chart as a guide in accomplishing *rational, programmed* change—for instance changing the reward system, who gets paid for what, regrouping and redesigning jobs and tasks to get quality—*if* the problem is mainly on the surface. The $64 million question is what to do if the problem is *not* amenable to surface treatment. What do you do if the problems aren't amenable to quick changes, rational explanation, and surface redesign of the organization? In other words, what do you do if your problems are deeply rooted in Cell 1?

From my experience, as strange as it may sound, you may have to adopt some change efforts that are founded on family therapy. As I outline them, I'm going *to caution you very, very carefully* that *none* of these suggestions should be tried *without* a highly skilled and trained specialist in organizational theory, as well as therapy, because the forces that we're playing around with are so powerful they can virtually blow up a situation.

One of the most fundamental discoveries to come from family therapy is that it is often virtually impossible to treat a single "sick" family member without diagnosing the dynamics and behavior of the family as a whole and its entire set of issues and problems. You can't fix just one part of a problem or system, because the defect or sickness is rarely located in just one part.

Please understand that I'm using the notion of a family as an analogy for an organization, because in many ways a family is like an organization and an organization is like a family. True, an organization may not seem to be as emotionally intense and as bound together as a family, or as long lasting, but in many cases it really is. Many of us hate to admit that we are more "married" to our jobs and careers than we are to our own families.

As strange as it sounds, research in family therapy has revealed that often a disturbed family actively *needs* one member to be sick in order to hold the family together. The reason is that the sick member functions as the designated sacrificial victim so that the other members can function somewhat normally. One person becomes the *receptacle* for the sickness of the whole system so that the others can function more "normally." Thus, the designated "sick person" is not always the truly "sick" member of the system.

If a family, like an organization, is deeply resistant to rational analyses of its problems, and hence to rationally designed programs of change, then the therapist or organizational change agent may have to engage in deeper efforts. In fact, we know not just from therapy alone but from our general experience that people naturally resist taking advice from others, even when they say they want it. The reason is natural. We avoid and resist advice so that we're not placed under the control of others.

My organization learned painfully that we fought not only the changes we needed to make but especially the therapist who pointed them out to us. What our organizational change agent/therapist finally did—and he didn't explain it to us in the beginning, he just did it—was to ally himself with us. He began to say, "Look, I've discovered that your beliefs really aren't wrong. In fact, I really think you should not only persist in what you've been doing, but even accentuate it."

Needless to say, I and a number of our top executives were flabbergasted by this. Later on, after we'd gone through it, the therapist explained that *at times you have to fight craziness with craziness in a system in order to get rid of it.* His aligning himself with our crazy behavior, which we were now convinced had to change, was met with extreme surprise and shock because we went to him in the first place knowing that we needed to change, and here he was telling us that we *didn't* need to change! In effect he was saying that *the very thing that was causing us pain needed to be intensified!*

Later on he told me what the analogy was to families. Sometimes, for instance, when dealing with a young child who takes on the symptoms of extreme anger or intense depression so that the mother and father can be free to have a semblance of a marriage, the therapist will write a letter or say to all the members of the family: "What a good child so-and-so is. What a good person he is to single himself out to sop up all the suffering in the family so that his mother and father can keep their marriage together. If anything, I think he ought to engage in more suffering so that they can have an even better marriage!"

Now, not in all cases, but in some, let me tell you what the reaction to this kind of change effort is. If there is strong resistance to change and hence to anyone promoting it, the organization is forced into changing itself by resisting the therapist! That is, if it resists the therapist, it is really engaged in resisting or changing itself; by rejecting the therapist it is then involved in rejecting the behavior with which the therapist has aligned himself.

In fact, let me tell you what the person we

hired did. *He not only intensified our symptoms, but he sat down and wrote out a deliberate
schedule so that the painful symptoms we were
experiencing could be produced on demand!* For
example, like you, we were caught up in blaming our workers. We had foremen and workers at
one another all over the place. We had different
groups just about ready to kill one another. What
the therapist did, paradoxically enough, was to
say, "Three times a week and *only* during those
three times, the different groups will engage in a
systematic program of blaming one another." In
fact, they not only had to schedule their behavior but they had to intensify their blame, that is,
blame each other four times as much as before.
I can tell you what happened. After a while, it all
became so ridiculous that we began to see what
we were doing. It wasn't one group or another
that was at fault or deserved blame, it was our
whole system. It's only when we began to understand this that we could really change ourselves.
In effect, we learned that if we could produce our
problems on demand and even intensify them,
then we also had it within our power to reduce
them!

But—but—I have to emphasize, this is a very
tricky and dangerous procedure, as dangerous
and tricky as change itself unless it's managed
by the right person, who knows what symptoms
to intensify in order to change the system. You
can't accomplish change in this way with every

kind of organization or by intensifying every bad symptom. As I've stressed repeatedly, do this with the wrong organization or symptom and you can literally destroy the system, not help it to get better.

Okay, let me close again by listing two sets of contrasting assumptions:

Inappropriate Assumptions for Accomplishing Deep Change

Appropriate Assumptions for Accomplishing Deep Change

1. The system wants to get rid of, be free of its problems.

1. The system wants to maintain its problems and in fact needs them in order to function; indeed it even assigns, consciously and unconsciously, different roles within the organization to play out its problems so that it can function and thus maintain itself. For example, some people are informally designated as victims, some as helpers, some as problem solvers, some as leaders, etc. Both the problems and the solutions thus help to maintain the set of roles, and vice versa.

2. The problems we face are not consciously chosen or deliberately designed by us; thus, they cannot be foreseen; they just come at us from the outside world.

2. The system in some sense actively chooses and even very cleverly and subtly designs the problems that it wants.

3. The system would be better off without its problems.

3. The system will not necessarily be better off without its problems if it is not given something else to focus and concentrate its energy on.

4. Solutions are designed to eliminate problems.

4. Solutions actually embody within them the power to maintain problems. In other words, to change a problem we need to change the solutions as well, because the solutions may just feed into the problems and keep them going. After all, the solutions are matched to the problems; the trouble is they may be so well matched that the "solutions" may actually reinforce and

even intensify the problems.

5. We cannot take charge and control our problems.

5. Not only can we take charge and control our problems with help and understanding, but we can learn either to intensify them or to reduce their intensity.

6. We have no reason to enjoy our problems nor do we have a right to.

6. We can sometimes learn to enjoy our problems.

7. Problems can be removed by being rational and "sensical."

7. Deep, persistent problems can only be removed by being in some sense rationally "nonsensical," i.e., "rational" in a deeper and broader sense than mere surface rationality.

Let me summarize with a couple of quotations from the great Austrian philosopher Ludwig Wittgenstein. I think he said it all far better than I ever could. The first is: "The problems of life are insoluble on the surface." The second is much longer:

Getting hold of the difficulty [the problem] *deep down* is what is hard.

38

Because if it [the problem] is grasped near the surface it simply remains the difficulty it was. It has to be pulled out by the roots; and that involves our beginning to think about these things in a new way. The change is as decisive as, for example, that from the alchemical to the chemical way of thinking. The new way of thinking is what is so hard to establish.

Once the new way of thinking has been established, the old problems vanish; indeed they become hard to recapture. For they go with our way of expressing ourselves and, if we clothe ourselves in a new form of expression, the old problems are discarded along with the old garment. (Ludwig Wittgenstein, *Culture and Value*. Translated by Peter Winch. Oxford: Basil Blackwell, 1980, p. 43)

MEMOS 5 & 6

Weird Connections: The Old Rules for Doing Business Have Changed Forever

TO: Bob Fountain

FROM: Steve Hart

DATE: June 2, 1988

SUBJECT: Help; I Think I'm Beginning to
          Understand!

It's *starting* to make sense to me. But . . . I still
can't say that I either understand or agree with
all of what you did. As powerful as it is—maybe
because it's *too* powerful—your way of thinking
about people is still too strange and counterintuitive for me. I'm afraid that I've become something like your client and I'm now in the position
of resisting you like you resisted your therapist!

I do sense, however, that underneath it all,
you're basically right. Our real problems have
never been on the surface. If they were, they
would have been amenable to simple, quick fixes
all along, and as a result, they would have been
solved long ago. The fact that they've been so
persistent proves that we've just been treating
symptoms and not the real problems themselves.
We've certainly not been dealing with the underlying causes that made them keep popping back
up no matter how much we tried to beat them
down.

If I really understand you, the therapist you
brought in was acting like a kind of judo master.

Instead of resisting or fighting you, he was in a way flowing with you. By doing so, he got you fighting your own problems instead of fighting him. Pretty clever!

But my God, Bob, what kind of world has it become where we can't treat problems directly? I think *this* is the real problem that all of us are facing even though most of us don't want to acknowledge it. What in God's name has happened to change the rather simple, straightforward world in which you and I grew up into one so full of complexity that it takes more than sheer cleverness or smarts to get by? I have some thoughts about this issue, since I've been thinking about it for quite some time. I'd like to share them with you as my contribution to our game of bouncing ideas back and forth.

I think that finally we may have reached the real issue that we need to discuss.

TO: Bob

FROM: Steve

DATE: June 12, 1988

SUBJECT: Weird Connections, or, Why the
Rules of the Game Have Changed!
Why Everything That Once Made for
Our Comparative Advantage Now
Makes for Our Comparative
Disadvantage

Let me share with you some ideas that I've been
toying with for some time. They have to do with
why the world we're facing is so different from
anything we've ever seen before. It's this very
background that makes me receptive to your
ideas regarding how to manage people even if
they aren't entirely comfortable or natural to me.
Indeed, I think it's this background against which
I'm framing all problems that makes the exchange
between us even more necessary.

   I think that the majority of managers and executives in this country are still operating from
what I would call the World War II or "simple machine" model of the world. Just prior to, during,
and certainly immediately after WWII, I think the
world operated according to a few basic principles that were decisively in our favor. The trouble
is that nearly every one of these advantages has

now vanished or diminished to the point that the conditions that made possible the overwhelming success of the U.S. business and economic system no longer operate.

What were these advantages? First, for a long time we could take for granted that we had cheap and abundant energy, labor, and raw materials that gave us superiority over most other countries in the world with regard to production and manufacturing capability. For example, if our labor force wasn't always cheaper than other countries', then certainly the cost of our energy and raw materials was. Second, the United States had such huge, unsaturated, internal domestic markets that for all practical purposes we could ignore the rest of the world; in effect, we didn't have to think globally and develop global marketing strategies. Our internal domestic markets were so big and so hungry for consumer goods, especially after WWII, that it seemed they would never become satiated.

At the same time, it used to take longer to develop products and to exhaust their life cycles. For example, thirty years ago it might have taken twenty to thirty years for a product such as a refrigerator to move through the cycle of its initial development and introduction to the market to its obsolescence, saturation, or "death." Also, during this era, in general only the elites, opinion leaders, and early adopters could purchase the initial versions of a product. Thus it took time for products to diffuse through to the rest of the population. All this made it relatively easy for businesses to plan for the birth, maturity, and even death of their products so that they could anticipate the orderly transition to production of new items.

Look at what's different today. The time between the introduction, maturity, and death of a product is shrinking to practically zero. How the hell can you plan for what to produce and sell under such conditions? It becomes almost impossible.

There were a few other factors operating that gave us our decisive advantage over other countries. In effect, the laws of comparative advantage formulated some 200 years ago by David Ricardo and his followers operated for a long time. These "laws" said that countries could produce only according to what nature had given them via natural resources or the raw talent of their populations. For example, if one country was blessed with a good grape-growing climate, then it was both naturally restricted to and competitive in producing wine. If, on the other hand, nature dictated that certain kinds of materials or animals for producing cloth prospered well in a certain country, then in effect nature had dictated that that country should stick to producing what it was endowed with and produced best.

Nearly all of this has changed today. Virtually any country can import the technology necessary to produce just about anything. In effect, countries today are no longer limited by what was seemingly a natural constraint in Ricardo's time; that is, you don't have to take the cards that nature has dealt you as inevitably limiting constraints for all time. For instance, the cost of transporting raw materials long distances from one country to another is not as significant today as it was a couple of hundred years ago. As a result, the factors limiting what a nation can produce are more a matter of technology than of raw materials.

When the cost of transporting goods and raw materials is no longer a major factor in production, when transporting huge volumes of information and data across national lines no longer represents a significant cost in time and dollars, and when information can be transmitted almost instantaneously, then the world has lost, once and for all, the natural buffering of distance among nations. Although most Americans may still think in isolationist terms because they're a long way from either Europe or the Pacific Rim, the world doesn't operate like that anymore. Information now crosses both oceans at lightning speed. As a result, it's much easier for foreign manufacturers to penetrate our markets than ever before. Even more significant, they can easily establish direct manufacturing and dealer distributorships on our home shores.

What I'm saying is that we've lost whatever

buffer we had built into our system. When we had huge, unsaturated domestic markets hungry for anything we could throw at them and consumers who all wanted the same things, we could get away with equally huge, bureaucratic organizations and production lines that were sloppy or inefficient. We could get away with friction and hostility among labor, management, government, and stockholders. The problem is that we can't get away with that any longer. We're competing with countries that make high-quality goods because they have forged close *alliances* among their employees, managers, governments, and shareholders. They may not be perfect alliances, but they stand in sharp contrast to our adversarial relationships.

In short, we were shielded from the rest of the world by temporary advantages that have now passed on to others.

Let me give you a concrete example that may help to make some of this clearer. I recently read an article on the front page of the Business section of the *Washington Post* that brought home to me, as forcefully as anything could, just how much our world has changed. The article had to do with the fact that the U.S. and the worldwide travel industry really took it "in the shorts" last year. Obviously, the threat of terrorism made travelers fearful of traveling abroad. That part of the reason for the travel industry's troubles we can readily understand. The next part of the article, though, really shook me and drove home once again why the world has changed so dramatically; that was the fact that travelers also stayed away from Europe because of the Chernobyl incident, that is, the fear of nuclear radiation.

Bob, imagine this scenario. Suppose that, say, three years ago we had assembled a small conference of fifty people in one room, twenty-five from the travel industry and twenty-five from the nuclear industry, and had said to them that a significant event would happen in the nuclear industry that would greatly affect the travel industry. You know what would have happened? Not only would both groups have looked at one another in complete surprise, but they would have looked at us as though we were crazy and had just descended from Mars.

The point is that the world is now governed by a condition of weird connections! *The most improbable events that you and I can think of can now crisscross and connect in strange and unpredictable ways, defying our ability to foresee or make sense of them.* There is no separation anymore between parts of the globe. In effect, everything is now local news.

The Chernobyl disaster shows how totally interconnected we've become. For instance, I understand it took about two weeks for the *physical* cloud of radiation from Chernobyl to encircle the earth and contaminate fish on opposite sides of the globe. But it took only a half a day for our *financial* markets to react to Chernobyl. The reason is that if the "bread basket" of the Soviet Union were knocked out of commission for God knows how long, what would that do to the futures for grain markets in our country? Our financial markets reacted almost instantaneously to Chernobyl because we're literally wired electronically to every event on the whole planet. Events like Chernobyl are capable of affecting the whole planet not only physically, but also electronically and financially. We've never before had the capability of affecting events like this. We are now more coupled to distant forces than we have ever been.

I read recently that since 1900 there have been twenty-eight major industrial accidents in the world of the kind now that took place in Bhopal. Chernobyl has increased the number to twenty-nine. "Major" indicates the deaths of at least fifty people. The estimates are that Chernobyl will exceed this number by hundreds if not thousands of deaths.

The clinker in the preceding statistic is that not only have there been twenty-nine major industrial accidents since 1900, but that half of these have occurred in the last eight years! The ante keeps going up—the disasters we are witnessing are bigger in scope, and the time between them is shrinking precipitously.

The whole structure of our world seems to

have changed. I doubt seriously that a poison-
ing incident of the kind represented by Tylenol®
would have happened some sixty years ago. The
kinds of accidents we had then were no less devastating to a particular community but the point
is that for the most part they were confined to
a particular community. A disaster like a mine
explosion could be catastrophic for a particular
community, but it wouldn't have affected a whole
region or a whole nation. The reason a Tylenol
incident can happen today is that we have the
mixed blessings of modern communications and
travel technology. Mass communication and mass
transportation make it possible for a single individual, a psychopath, to get on a plane and visit
five cities in a day. Thus when somebody calls
a company with a product-tampering threat we
implement a nationwide recall of products unless we can determine that the tampering threat,
if indeed it was real to begin with, is confined to
a particular locale or a particular batch of products. This, I submit to you, is very different from
anything that happened or could have happened
sixty years ago.

No wonder paradox operates in today's world.
No wonder things aren't as straightforward as
they once were. No one can foresee the complex interconnectedness of all things. Even
though one starts out assuming that what one is
doing is good, it can have adverse effects. Things
are now so complex that actions that seem good

can lead to the complete opposite of what was intended.

Okay, let me try to play your game. Let me summarize as you've been doing with two contrasting sets of assumptions which I think get at what's going on and describe the differences between the old world prior to and just after World War II, and the new world that has developed since the 1970s:

The Old Organizing Assumptions or Rules for Doing Business Before 1970	*The New Organizing Assumptions or Rules for Doing Business Since 1970*
1. U.S. domestic markets are so big that manufacturers can safely ignore the rest of the world; U.S. markets will never be saturated for traditional consumer products and U.S. consumer tastes will always be homogeneous.	**1.** No markets anywhere can now be safely ignored. To compete anywhere one must be prepared to compete everywhere. U.S. markets have become virtually saturated for traditional consumer goods, and tastes have become differentiated into distinctive market niches.
2. The raw materials of the underdeveloped countries can serve indefinitely as strategic reserves to the U.S.	**2.** The underdeveloped countries have learned to harness their reserves to their own strategic advantage

economy and can be called on at will at prices below prevailing world standards.

3. There is enormous slack in the U.S. economic and social system, for instance, in the form of cheap energy, labor, raw materials, and huge domestic markets that are safe from foreign competition and intrusion. As a result, the U.S. can get away with sloppy, inefficient management.

4. World markets will be dominated by one or two top players for relatively long periods of time.

5. Bureaucracy is the best form of organization; standardization and mass production are the keys to success.

through the use of the latest technology.

3. There is little or no slack available to any one player in the world market; if anything, the slack we once enjoyed has now passed to other countries. The U.S. no longer possesses the advantages of cheap labor, and its huge domestic markets are no longer safe from foreign intrusion.

4. There is no more long-term domination of world markets by any one player, although those that understand the "new rules" of the world economy can gain significant short-term advantage.

5. Bureaucracy is the worst form for competing effectively in a global economy. Flexibility and extreme adaptability to

shifting markets and consumer tastes are the new keys, coupled with high-quality products and services. Hence, new forms of organization are evolving rapidly.

6. There is little if any connection between distant, improbable events.

6. Any number of events located anywhere on the Earth's surface can now interconnect in strange ways.

I've summarized all these so-called prior decisive advantages in a table.

Decisive Advantages?

1. Huge, unsaturated domestic markets
2. Relatively cheap energy, labor, raw materials
3. Large distances: cost of transporting information, materials, products
4. Large, bureaucratic organizations
5. Inefficient management
6. Inefficient labor
7. Adversarial relations
8. Long lead times
9. Stable/proprietary technology
10. Stable markets/demand
11. Homogeneity of consumer tastes
12. Edge in key technology
13. Simple/placid environment
14. Disregard of global marketing
15. Decoupled world economies
16. Long life cycles
17. Bigger is better (scale)
18. No need to modernize

In a word, the old world in which we lived was a protected cocoon. We don't live in that kind of world anymore. It was great while it lasted, but because it was so simple it didn't prepare us at all for the time when the bubble would burst. That's why our quality problem is now so critical. We can't get away with producing low-quality goods if we're going to compete in this changed environment.

The question I have for you is what rules and principles you evolved to manage in this new environment. I'd like your thoughts.

MEMO 7

The Failure of Success: The Life Cycle of Assumptions

TO: Steve Hart

FROM: Bob Fountain

DATE: July 10, 1988

SUBJECT: The Failure of Success

The best and easiest way I can explain to you
how I manage in today's environment is by
illustrating the approach I use in thinking through
complex issues. I'm going to illustrate it as systematically as I can in terms of one particular industry, the U.S. automobile industry. However,
I hope it will become clear that much of what
I'm going to say is applicable to any industry.
Only the specifics will change, and many of the
specifics are generalizable. What's now apparent to me as a result of your previous memo is
that I've been taking for granted the very changed
nature of the environment that you described so
well. I never saw it as clearly as before.
    I want to give you two treatments of what I
think were the critical assumptions from which
the U.S. automobile industry operated. The first
set comes primarily from a number of books I've
read recently on the history of the industry in
general. The second comes from a study that was
done of General Motors in particular.
    Both studies indicate that the life cycle of the
automobile industry's critical premises was no

more than sixty years at best. From roughly 1910 to 1970, the assumptions directing the industry were not only valid, but they made for the overwhelming success of one of the most successful industries the world has ever known. But then almost overnight, in the span of some five to ten years, they virtually collapsed. They became invalid and so out of touch with reality that the industry almost went down the tubes—for good.

The bottom line of my approach is this: *Know the critical assumptions from which you have been operating, and monitor the environment carefully for signals that indicate that those assumptions may either be reversing themselves or collapsing.* When they begin to collapse, act decisively to prepare your organization for the new policies that are in accord with the new assumptions that are developing. (Remember our very first discussions about change?)

Steve, look at the attached list of what I call "the unwritten rules of the American automobile industry." Notice that I have listed them in two columns. Column 1 shows my "street interpretations" of the more professional or scholarly wording of these assumptions.

Look down the list. You can see that the assumptions are so intertwined with technological, human, social, and organizational factors that it's literally impossible to say where one leaves off and the other begins. In effect, they constitute a complete *social contract* for running the car

The Unwritten Rules of the American Automobile Industry

STRAIGHT TALK	PROFESSIONAL TALK
1. An easy, short childhood is the best preparation for adulthood and maturity.	It was a distinct advantage that by about 1930 the modern car industry was firmly established, its competitive practices well understood, its major product design features firmly locked into place, etc.
2. We are stable now and forevermore; the broader world is stable.	The competitive dynamics and basic business of automobile production is essentially stable and well known.
3. "They love us" (i.e., our products); they're loyal, won't switch; we can take them for granted; we can assume consumer stability.	The tastes of U.S. car buyers are standardized and stable; thus, except for yearly styling changes, we do not have to make radical or substantial changes in our product. U.S. car buyers will not demand a new type of car that we have never built in large volume before.
4. Nothing new will be invented that will radically shake up our product; essentially, we know it all; the stability of car technology can be taken for granted.	The design/production of future cars will not require fundamentally new manufacturing processes or technologies.
5. Our focus need not be broader than the driver; a restricted focus of innovation can be assumed.	Innovations relating to driver comfort are more important than fundamental technical innovations in the basic product.
6. Don't change until forced to; resist, deny change; put your major energies into denial and resistance.	We can succeed by not spending money on fundamental innovations until forced to by governmental regulatory agencies, foreign competition, consumers, etc.

Memo 7

The Unwritten Rules of the American Automobile Industry

STRAIGHT TALK	PROFESSIONAL TALK
7. Get your priorities wrong; innovation can take a back seat to efficiency.	Because of GM's dominant industry strategy (under A.P. Sloan), based on clever marketing to different demographic segments of the population and frequent style changes, technical innovation was subordinated to efficiency in production; i.e., efficiency is more important than innovation.
8. Keep getting your priorities wrong; good labor relations can take a back seat to efficiency.	Efficiency in production is more important than good labor relations; good labor relations are not important to efficiency.
9. We're so big and powerful, smug and secure that we can shut out the whole world; we can charge and pass on anything we want to our customers. So what if we're arrogant?	Foreign competition will never be significant; therefore, U.S. car makers will not be prevented from passing the higher costs of production necessary to keep up with the competition on to consumers.
10. Since we don't need much innovation, we can finance whatever we want to.	The capital and debt capacity required to finance whatever innovations are required will be readily available.
11. Managers don't need challenge in their work; the restricted focus/nature of managerial work can be assumed.	As the business of car making became well understood, not only did managerial work become routine, but it was desirable that it did so. The challenge of managerial work was not necessary to the long-term success of the industry.
12. If you want to get tunnel vision, then you have to reward	An extremely handsome bonus system that rewards top

62

The Unwritten Rules of the American Automobile Industry

STRAIGHT TALK	PROFESSIONAL TALK
it. We are masters at creating a system for producing managerial myopia.	management for short-term thinking is not hazardous to the long-term interests of the entire industry.
13. Workers don't need challenge in their jobs; the restricted focus/nature of all jobs can be assumed.	Workers are willing to trade money for challenge in their jobs.
14. Keep everyone small-minded and uninvolved.	It is not necessary to engage most employees in the larger purposes of the business.
15. Don't rock the boat; don't bite the hand that feeds you; these rules pertain to the unwritten culture of the industry.	It is not in the interests of top managers to tamper with the system that has promoted them. It is not necessary for top management to look at the big or whole picture.
16. We don't need constant informal parties as they do in Silicon Valley.	It is not necessary to foster an industry-wide culture of innovation, intense competition between companies, informal sharing of information, entrepreneurism, and the intense cycling of executives between firms.
17. We've discovered *the* principles of organization for all time.	Not only is the organizational structure of U.S. car makers appropriate for its time, if not all time, but it is well suited to responding to changing governmental policies, consumer tastes, and foreign competition.
18. No one, including our-selves, can teach us anything about good organization; we	Despite GM's great success due to its early organizational structure under Alfred P.

The Unwritten Rules of the American Automobile Industry

STRAIGHT TALK	PROFESSIONAL TALK
resist learning anything even from ourselves.	Sloan, Ford was correct to resist the professionalization of its upper management for so long, and Chrysler was correct to resist adopting GM's structure of high differentiation and high integration. In other words, U.S. car makers had nothing significant to learn from one another regarding the design of their respective organizational structures.

business. All of them assume that nearly everyone connected with the system had no need for more than a fragmented, compartmentalized understanding of the business.

They also assumed that customer preferences were well understood and that customers really didn't want very sophisticated cars. All of these things may appear stupid to us now, but they weren't for a long, long time. Indeed, they *were true* for almost sixty years.

The failure of the automobile industry was the failure to see that when these assumptions began to change, the industry needed to base its practices on new assumptions. The difficulty is that when a set of rules makes sense for so long, it's almost impossible to change them because they begin to take on the character of eternal truths. (Notice that we're cycling back to our very first memos dealing with change.)

The moral is that *the U.S. auto industry didn't fail because it was a failure from day one but because it was a success for so long, and it took its success for granted.* The industry thought it had found the magic formula for success for all time when all it had found was a particular set of conditions, as embodied in its key assumptions, that were good for a limited period of time.

I repeat: *The failure of the U.S. auto industry is not the "failure of failure"; instead, it is the "failure of success."* Like most industries, instead of changing when it needed to, it responded by investing even more in its old practices, that is, it reinforced its old assumptions even more. Instead of changing, it did even more of the same.

Now look at the next set of assumptions that pertain specifically to GM. The first column outlines the generic set of issues that GM, like all organizations, had to manage. The middle column describes the old operating assumptions. In many ways, they repeat the assumptions in the previous table, but I wanted to list them again in order to lay out the new operating assumptions that I believe GM as well as every member of the automobile industry now has to abide by.

From the beginning of our dialogue, I've been trying to say that as CEOs we have a dual job. You and I are not just makers of products—although of course we do that—but

Memo 7

General Motors: Assumptions and Counter-Assumptions

GENERIC ISSUES	OLD OPERATING ASSUMPTIONS	NEW OPERATING ASSUMPTIONS
1. What business are we basically in? Who has basic control of the organization?	1. GM is in the business of making money, not cars. (The accounting and finance people took over control of the organization after the industry passed its start-up phase, which was run by people who wanted to make cars.)	1. GM is primarily in the business of making quality cars, not money. Any organization that forgets its purpose for going into business in the first place will not achieve one of its fundamental financial objectives. (The engineers and the accounting/ finance people should share control.)
2. What must our posture toward innovation be?	2. Success comes not from techno- logical leadership but from having the resources to quickly adopt innovations successfully intro- duced by others.	2. We cannot give up technological leadership in a world that is more competi- tive than ever. We no longer have the luxury of time in a more complex environment.
3. How does the customer view our product?	3. Cars are primarily status symbols. Styling is therefore more important than quality to buyers who are, after all, going to trade up every other year.	3. Quality and styling are equally important in a more competitive market where even the cheapest car is expensive by past standards and where the competition is able to produce well- crafted and stylish products.

General Motors: Assumptions and Counter-Assumptions

GENERIC ISSUES	OLD OPERATING ASSUMPTIONS	NEW OPERATING ASSUMPTIONS
4. How much control do we actually have over our outside environment? How much can we really insulate ourselves from it?	4. The American car market is isolated from the rest of the world. Foreign competitors will never gain more than 15% of the domestic market.	4. The American car market will never be as isolated from the rest of the world as it once was. Foreign competition is here to stay, and it will always be significant.
5. What are the basic resources this organization needs in order to do business, and how available will they be in the future?	5. Energy will always be cheap and abundant.	5. Energy will never again be cheap or abundant, even though it may be held artificially low for what seems like an indefinite period of time; it will fluctuate enormously.
6. What skills and education of person-nel do we need to presume in order to do business?	6. Workers do not have an important impact on produc-tivity or product quality.	6. Even with auto-mation, worker attitudes and skills at all levels are more important than ever.
7. How isolated are we from the shifting concerns of our customers?	7. The consumer movement does not represent a significant portion [of] the American public.	7. Given the rising costs of all products and the increasing concern with the environment, there will continue to be some organizations that will represent these concerns. Any organization that ignores them is dangerously deluding itself.

General Motors: Assumptions and Counter-Assumptions

GENERIC ISSUES	OLD OPERATING ASSUMPTIONS	NEW OPERATING ASSUMPTIONS
8. What is our attitude toward the government? Who do we perceive to be our natural enemies, our allies; why?	8. The government is the enemy. It must be fought tooth and nail every inch of the way.	8. The government is a significant factor in the environment, and as such it must be dealt with whether one likes it or not. It is too easy to blame others for our problems.
9. Which types of controls are appropriate?	9. Strict, centralized financial controls are the secret to good administration.	9. Compulsive financial controls are the cause and effect of bad administration. There is all the difference in the world between a financial system that *controls* an organization and one that *enables* it to do what it wants to and should do.
10. How closed off is our organization to new ideas from the outside? How open, how trusting are we? What's our organizational culture like?	10. Managers should be developed from the inside.	10. The culture of an organization should be continually assessed to ensure that it has not become a closed system resistant to new ideas.

we're also the prime keepers and formulators of the assumptions of our organizations and even of our industries. I can summarize this in a kind of formula:

The quality of our assumptions multiplied by the quality of our production processes equals the quality of our performance as a firm times the quality of our delivered products. As an "equation," it looks like this:

Quality of our assumptions	$\times$	Quality of our production processes	$=$	Quality of our performance as a firm	$\times$	Quality of our delivered products

$$\text{Quality}^{\text{SQUARED}} = \text{Quality}^{\text{SQUARED}}$$

You need quality at every point along the entire process to get quality at the end. I can't really separate any of the factors in this equation. You might call the quality of our assumptions the "soft" part of management and the quality of our production processes the "hard" part, but I don't think the words "hard" and "soft" really make any sense in today's world. I've never liked them as terms anyway. I'd rather say that we're dealing with the importance of one set of factors times the importance of another set of factors, which equals importance^{squared}; importance^{squared} equals something highly critical. It doesn't matter whether a factor is "hard" or "soft" as long as it's important. It's importance that counts, not "hardness" or "softness." I'm stressing this because I think too many of us get caught with one or the other when it's both that count. And

69

if both count equally, it doesn't really matter what you call them except for the fact that too many otherwise intelligent people get misdirected by simple-minded labels that are no longer appropriate.

What good is the distinction "soft" versus "hard" if every so-called "hard" factor depends upon a set of "soft" assumptions? Did the space shuttle Challenger blow up because of the failure of the "hard" O-ring (i.e., technology) or because of the "soft" communications and organization breakdown (i.e., human factors)? It failed because of both. That's why the distinction is irrelevant at best and stupid and misleading at worst. The distinction diverts us from recognizing that both are important no matter what they're called.

Look at the right side of the equation. The quality of performance means not only how well our organization does on "the bottom line" measured in dollars but how our people feel about our organization, for instance, how well our organization communicates and provides the right information to the right people so that we can achieve the quality of our final delivered products.

So what's my approach? Let me say it once again: Monitor as carefully as you can *all* the critical components of your system—whether they be technology, people, politics, vested interest groups, general assumptions in our broader culture, etc.—and *bring to the surface all the assumptions you're making about every one of them; then do everything in your power to ask whether there is an opposite, competing assumption that makes more sense for today's world.*

We are the monitors, the keepers, the leaders, and the shapers of our organization's assumptions. If we don't challenge our most fundamental beliefs when they are in dire need of revision, then who will? Will it be our competition who, unfettered by our history, can begin anew where we cannot?

I should note that once I have identified the key assumptions on which my business is predicated, I then sort them on the chart on page 72.

The assumptions in Cells I and II are the most important to the success of my business. In Cell II are those assumptions which are known to be either true or false. Those in Cell I are the most critical of all because they are highly uncertain; that is, they are as likely to be true as false. A good example is the cost of energy. It seems that no matter what number you state for the cost of energy, it's as likely to be false as it is to be true. Energy prices are a crap-shoot.

Memo 7

Certain
(Known to Be Either True or False)

```
          III          |          II



Unimportant ──────────┼────────── Highly Critical


          IV           |          I
```

Problematic
(As Likely to Be
True as False)

The key point is that you can't wait for everything in Cell I to move up to II before you take
action, because by the time it's clear that it's
either true or false for you it will also be clear to
your competition. You will have lost whatever advantage you might have seized by acting quickly.
You've got to act on the basis that the assumptions which fall in Cell I are critical to the success
of your venture. You've got to formulate the best
plans you can, given the deep uncertainty of the
assumptions in Cell I.

Welcome to the wonderful world of high uncertainty! I know of no better way of grappling with it than this.

MEMOS 8 & 9

Persistent Doubts

TO: Bob Fountain

FROM: Steve Hart

DATE: August 10, 1988

SUBJECT: Persistent Doubts

- The issue is not whether *I'm* convinced of the importance of knowing assumptions.
- I'm convinced!
- The issue I've been struggling with is this: How do you convince *others* that they must examine *their* assumptions.
- What assumptions do you have to make in order to know that you've reached the right assumptions?
- I think what really bothers me is the whole process you use. Even though I find it very amenable, it's so personal, so squishy, so fuzzy, and so open-ended that I'm not sure whether most people have the temperament to practice it, though I can appreciate what it's trying to accomplish.
- Perhaps this is where I'm the weakest. For me, the issue always keeps coming back to people. How do you involve others in a process that you take to be so natural? Is everyone suited to the way that you and I

think? I've tried to get others involved in what I do, and it just doesn't seem to work. Maybe I just don't know how to explain it to them or how to motivate them to want to do it.

TO: Steve Hart

FROM: Bob Fountain

DATE: October 15, 1988

SUBJECT: Persistent Doubts

I'm the first to admit that no procedure is best for everyone. Temperament *is* one of the biggest factors in the acceptance, use, and understanding of any procedure. Before you give up altogether and want to abandon what we've been talking about, even though I know that deep down you agree with it, let me try to explain it in a way that may help you to overcome some of the barriers and natural resistance that everyone has toward any kind of process.

It's entirely fair on your part to ask me what assumptions I have to make in order to get at my business assumptions. But in asking this you're already, as you know, affirming the critical role that assumptions play whether they're easy to get at or not. So as soon as you ask me this question, you're already playing my game. Indeed, you're already showing that you've learned how to play the game rather well. You're trapped in a paradox, to recall one of our earlier discussions.

Of course, the whole process is squishy, fuzzy, personal, open-ended, etc., but that's not necessarily the fault of the process. Rather, it's the nature of this new world, and you've described it as well as anyone I know. *The world* is squishy, fuzzy, personal, open-ended, and all those supposedly bad things.

Do you think that I don't struggle any more than you do to motivate my people? Do you think just because I've studied psychology and used consultants who were accomplished in psychology that I have fewer problems with people? Do you really think it's any easier for me to manage people just because of a process I can explain to you? I wish it were.

Every method, no matter how objective it seems on the surface, has a personal element to it. If Western culture hadn't been so brainwashed with the idea that natural science is always objective, then we'd have a lot less difficulty in adjusting to today's world. You ought to read some of the eye-opening accounts that have appeared in recent years on the extremely personal and even subjective elements that have always been present in science.

You and I can't help it that the world has become so complex that it's now necessary to get beneath the surface of things in order to deal with the underlying premises on which we base our daily actions. Whether assumptions and the world are fuzzy, squishy, or not is frankly quite irrelevant. Our job is to deal with the world no matter what it is like. *A CEO's job is precisely to handle the anxiety that goes with the uncertainty that comes out of the unknown.* This is true whether the anxiety comes from us or from our subordinates. What else are we paid for?

For this reason, I trust the details of my everyday business to my subordinates so that I can monitor the fuzzy issues. This doesn't mean that I don't get involved in details; we both know the trouble you can get in by not knowing what your subordinates are doing. (The "Iran-Contra affair": need I say more?) But I only evaluate the details against our core assumptions and I use the details to check on their continued validity.

(As an aside, one of the chief reasons most of the subordinates in both our organizations will not make it to the top is that they can't handle the anxiety we've been talking about. Over the years a number of my subordinates have approached me, asking either whether they have what it takes to be a leader right now or whether I could train them. Although in many cases I have known the answer before putting them through what I've been discussing with you, I nevertheless give them the chance to try out the process. The hard fact is that most of them fall by the wayside. They aren't mentally or emotionally tough enough to meet the challenges.

(In this sense, I have to laugh at so much that has been written about leadership lately. We get the charismatic thing all out of proportion. Of course charisma is vitally important, I think it's an essential ingredient. But I think we make too much of people like Lee Iacocca when we turn them into near gods. You know what leadership really is? It's all this damn stuff that we've been talking about. For example, one of the things that is talked about almost as much as charisma is the need for vision in leadership. I couldn't agree more. But where does vision come from? Does it fall off trees? Does it descend from the gods? Hell, no! It emerges from the ability to see the overall theme that ties together all the critical premises that you and I have been surfacing, that pertain to where the world is now heading.)

I'm repeating myself because it's so important to get this absolutely straight. We don't have the luxury of waiting for everything to become a "hard" fact before we take action, because by the time it's become a fact for us, that is, perfectly obvious, it will also have become so for our competition, and we will have lost whatever decisive advantage we might have gained by acting early.

There are ways to get a grip on this uncertainty and anxiety. One of the most effective that I've found is to involve my key associates in the whole process. Do you think that I or any one person could do all of this alone? My God, man, I may be arrogant, but I'm not that stupid. (How stupid am I? That's another discussion.)

I regularly convene my top associates to examine our key premises. We find it helpful to break into three groups. On any complex issue, such as how we're going to compete in foreign mar-

kets, each group agrees to explore and defend
a radically different policy, so that while we may
not be able to examine all options, we can feel
that we've at least looked at the issue from three
very different perspectives and thus span the al-
ternatives. This way, we don't put all our policy
options into one basket.

After we've formulated the three differing
policies that we think need to be explored, we
then work *backwards* from each policy to see
what critical underlying assumptions we need to
make in order to support each policy. After we've
elicited the typically ten to fifteen critical assumptions needed to support, defend, or attack any
policy, we then debate the respective merits of
each assumption. We also place those assumptions on the grid I showed you in my last memo.
In this way, we can literally *see* what we're debat-
ing; we can get a precise grip on how and why
we differ. We can see, in other words, our differing belief systems.

The end result is the stripping away of everything inessential to the debate to get to the typically five to seven really key assumptions that
we need to check out through further market research before we make a decision as to which
policy should gain our unwavering support. If
we don't have the luxury of conducting market
research, we have to go with our best judgment
calls, but at least we feel we know more precisely
the critical unknowns upon which we are basing

our decisions. We then monitor our decisions very carefully. As soon as we get any evidence that the assumptions upon which our decisions were made are not panning out, we adjust them as quickly as we can.

If I knew a better procedure for real-world complex decisions, I'd be using it. I'm sure we both realize that the world is so much more complex than the rubbish they teach in business schools. They don't present the students with real problems there. They present canned exercises, "canned" because they're all preformulated and predigested. Even the so-called case method doesn't really prepare people for the real world, because not only are real cases much fuzzier, but each of the many parties involved in a real case has a different view of what the case is to begin with and what facts and evidence he'd include in it. It's like the old Japanese movie, *Rashomon,* where each of the characters involved had a completely different view of the events that unfolded. The only way I know to sort through this is to explore assumptions and get them out in the open so we can see *explicitly* what different people are assuming about the world.

You asked what the fundamental beliefs are that underlie my investigation of assumptions. They are as follows: The process of uncovering assumptions is so important, so critical, that it cannot be entrusted to any one person or group in an organization. As a result, at least three groups have to be given the explicit assignment to explore and to debate key assumptions in an open, give-and-take arena. In a word, I believe that more good comes out of a procedure based on controlled, productive *conflict* than out of quick and easy agreement.

I don't want "Yes" men and women around me. I encourage my people to challenge me, but boy if they are going to do so, then they had better get to the point by really zeroing in on what's critical. I believe that continually taking my people through such a process trains them to do this. As a result, we're constantly talking about our assumptions. We literally have a war room where our assumptions are written on a board, those we believe our competition is operating from, those the whole industry is operating from, and so forth.

In the end, though, no matter how much I lean on and involve my key associates, the final heat of whatever decision I make is mine. I have to lead the group to the best *synthesis* we can come to at any particular time. After we've heard all the debate, I encourage everybody to say, "Okay, what's the best we can now do out of the various options that we've presented?"

But Steve, I can't just keep saying this to you. It's time for you to try it. I can pass on books for you to read that have helped me refine the process and understand it better, but at some point you've got to make the decision whether it's right for you or not. Please let me know what you decide to do and how it works out.

I'm reminded of a story that is attributed to Socrates. Apparently a young lad approached Socrates with the request that he teach him. Socrates took the lad down to the sea and began to walk out deeper and deeper until the water was just about over the boy's head. With that, he pushed the boy's head down under the water and kept it there until he was struggling to breathe. When the boy finally reached the surface and was gasping for breath, Socrates turned to him and said, "When your desire to learn is as strong as your desire to breathe, *then and only then* can I teach you." I think the same applies to both of us. Only when our desire to try something new is that strong can we overcome the anxiety that such change always brings.

Steve, if I've been too hard on you, I apologize. But it's not you in particular that I'm mad at. It's all of us. American business has been operating in a dream world for too long. Why are most of our biggest corporations in trouble? They don't know how or don't want to do what we've been talking about. Consider the following as evidence:

Urgency and frank self criticism are novel for GM—and long overdue. Until this year, *two sustaining beliefs* [my emphasis] have shaped the company's actions. The first was that money and technology could solve all problems. The second was that GM has been getting better and better—the proof being that this year's GM cars are always nicer than last year's, or so it has appeared to GM, which for decades has tended to look no further than its navel in making such judgments. Now events have shattered the old *assumptions* [my emphasis], pressing home the limits of technology and rudely demonstrating that the real competition, and the real standards of excellence, are found outside General Motors. Most unsettling of all, not only are the Japanese and Europeans leaving GM in the dust but so too are Ford and Chrysler, those once scorned domestic competitors that had to run for their lives several years ago. (Anne B. Fisher, "GM Is Tougher Than You Think," *Fortune,* November 10, 1986, p. 56.)

I rest my case!

MEMOS 10, 11, 12, & 13

Crisis Management: What Kind of Crazy World Has It Become?

TO: Steve

FROM: Bob

DATE: November 10, 1988

SUBJECT: Crisis Management

Managing and dealing with people may be your
greatest source of anxiety. Mine, paradoxically,
is managing all the uncertainty that comes with
today's environment. One reason I was so hard
on you in my last memo is that even with the
best of methods for dealing with uncertainty, I
often still feel overwhelmed by it. I am the first
one to admit that there's no perfect method for
containing all the uncertainty that goes with
today's environment.

I have an issue that literally scares the hell out
of me and for which I can use all your conceptual
skills. I'm sure you've become aware, like everyone else, of the increased crisis potential of all
organizations. I'm talking about not only a Bhopal
and a Chernobyl but a Tylenol as well. Lately I've
begun to worry about all the crises that could
strike our organization. What drives me up the
wall is I'm not sure what we should be doing in
this area. Here's where I could really use your advice. Do you have any thoughts about crisis management?

TO: Bob

FROM: Steve

DATE: November 15, 1988

SUBJECT: Crisis Management

Managers who aren't scared about the increased disaster potential of organizations and who aren't putting some kind of plan and operational mechanisms in place to handle crises are so out of touch with reality that they are almost guaranteeing their chances of having a major crisis. As anyone knows from just reading the newspaper, the largest crises in recent years have become household words. I'm referring to the ones that you mentioned in your last memo: the Tylenol poisonings, the Bhopal disaster, the Chernobyl nuclear disaster, and the explosion of the Challenger space shuttle. Each of these catastrophes was an example of the worst of its kind. Thus, Tylenol represents the worst case to date of a nationwide produce-tampering incident. Bhopal was the largest industrial accident in history. Chernobyl was the largest nuclear accident. Finally, the destruction of the space shuttle was more than just the loss of a vehicle and seven lives; it threatened to cancel our entire manned space program.

As you hinted, for every one of these headline disasters, there are countless others that don't make the news but may be just as devastating to an organization. My colleagues and I recently commissioned an outside group to evaluate our disaster potential. They identified at least nineteen different types to which we were vulnerable:

1. Major product defects
2. Major plant/equipment defects
3. Major industrial accidents
4. Major computer breakdowns
5. Hostile takeovers
6. On-site sabotage/product tampering
7. Off-site sabotage/product tampering
8. Counterfeiting
9. False rumors, malicious slander
10. Bribery, price fixing
11. Sexual harassment
12. Terrorism
13. Executive kidnapping
14. Poor or faulty operator training
15. Copycat threats
16. Recalls
17. Boycotts
18. Loss of proprietary information
19. Misinformation/miscommunication

The motley nature of this list is itself a significant indicator of what we're up against. Clearly it's the height of folly and irresponsibility for any organization not to have planned for the occurrence of *at least one* major disaster from the above list, but how can any organization guard against or plan for all nineteen and even more? Individuals and organizations just don't have the intellectual, financial, and human resources to devote their energies equally to every one of these crises. Which crises, therefore, should an organization concentrate its energies and resources on? Is there any way to select on a *rational, systematic,* and *comprehensive* basis which crises an organization should prepare for and which, on the other hand, it can safely neglect?

Based upon recent research conducted by the outside group we brought in, we were convinced that there were some ways to put crisis plans on a more rational basis. I'm sure you can appreciate just how critical this is, since recently all kinds of players have been hopping on the crisis management bandwagon. Thus, for instance, PR specialists have developed quite a business for themselves by emphasizing who should communicate with the media and how they should do it during the heat of a crisis. Although the best PR firms emphasize the importance of media training *before* a crisis occurs, they often come on the scene after the fact. As a result, they largely neglect what an organization should be doing beforehand to prevent crises from occurring in the first place.

By the same token, various other experts such as security analysts and engineering firms all emphasize various fragmented pieces of the crisis management puzzle. No one puts it into a comprehensive framework in a coherent fashion. Let me get back to you shortly with two frameworks that were developed in conjunction with the researchers who assisted us in formulating an overview of crisis management. The first is based on the idea of a *crisis portfolio.* The second consists of a *process model of crisis management;* it lays out in a systematic fashion the phases that must be managed before, during, and after a major crisis of any kind.

TO: Bob

FROM: Steve

DATE: December 1, 1988

SUBJECT: Why Every Organization Needs a
Crisis Portfolio!

Let me describe briefly the concept of a crisis portfolio that I mentioned in my last memo.
As part of the research activities of the outside
group we brought in, they conducted a survey of
the public affairs officers of the *Fortune* 1000 corporations. They asked them basically two things:
How many incidents, out of the nineteen crises
(plus a few more) that I listed in my last memo,
had their organization experienced in the last
three years: Out of twenty or so, how many preventive actions that could be used to blunt potential
crises was their organization undertaking?

Without boring you with all the details, let me
get to the heart of the results. Take a look at Figures 1 and 2. Figures 1 and 2 are based on some
fancy statistical analyses (factor analysis, multi-
dimensional scaling, etc.) of the basic frequencies
of (1) incidents (crises) that the organizations
had experienced in the last three years, and (2)
preventive actions that they were undertaking to
blunt and cope with potential crises.

Figure 1 shows that crises can be grouped

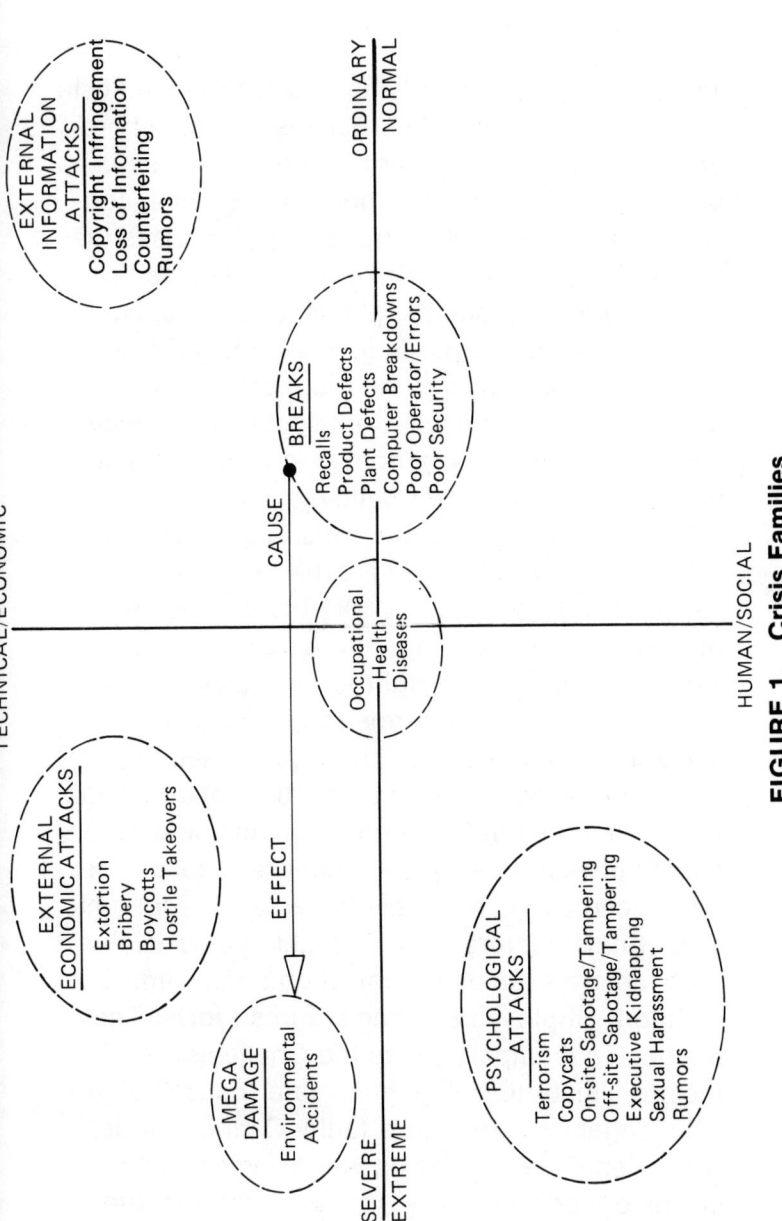

FIGURE 1. Crisis Families

97

according to their underlying structural similarity in certain groups or families. That is, the members of a particular family bear more than just a surface similarity to one another. For instance, consider the family labeled Breaks. All the crises that fall into this family consist of either defects or breakdowns in products, plants, packages, equipment, and even people (e.g., operators). For another, consider Psycho. All the members of this family consist of extreme, antisocial acts directed against corporations, products, consumers, executives, employees, their families, etc.

Note especially that the horizontal dimension is labeled "severity" because the crises on the left-hand side of Figure 1 fall outside the range of normal, everyday, rational human behavior, whereas those on the right are more easily understood and handled in terms of normal, everyday, societal institutions (e.g., the legal system) or scientific/technical knowledge, such as plant design.

Also notice that the vertical dimension differentiates between those crises that are "caused" or influenced by (1) relatively impersonal, economic, or technical factors, and (2) highly personal, human factors such as organizational miscommunication, employee sabotage, and so forth. This dimension is important, as the Challenger explosion illustrated. The immediate "cause" of the Challenger disaster was a faulty O-ring, that is, a poor engineering design which led to a catastrophic technical break. However, the real precipitating cause and underlying source of the accident was a faulty bureaucratic organization which deliberately blocked repeated warning signals (these were in the form of memos, reproduced in the *Report of the President's Commission on the Space Shuttle Challenger Accident*). These signals warned in no uncertain terms that unless the O-ring was corrected a tragedy was virtually guaranteed. As I will discuss later, virtually all crises, before they actually occur, leave a persistent trail of signals announcing their imminent occurrence. Hence, it is important not only to attend to these signals but to put in place an organizational mechanism that will notice them in the first place and act upon them in the second.

For now, however, the point is that nearly all crises involve a combination of factors from each of the families in Figure 1. For instance, in virtually all cases a combination of technical/economic and human/social factors will be involved and will contribute to the "final big crisis" that an organization experiences. (As an aside, I think that recognizing this, more than anything else, has convinced me of the importance of the "people dimension" in business. But then I've always been convinced of this. I've just lacked the insight and the detailed skills for handling this dimension properly.)

For this reason alone, I believe that every organization should develop a *crisis portfolio*. That is, it should pick *at least one* crisis from each of the families in Figure 1 against which to guard itself. In this way, if the members of each family bear some relationship to one another, then preparing for at least one crisis in each family confers some preparation for each of the others. In this way, an organization can at least minimally cover itself. I should emphasize that crisis planning is not the preparation of a thick set of plans which sit on a shelf but rather a process of continually asking "what if" questions. What if multiple crises hit us simultaneously; what are we prepared to do? Are we trained both intellectually and emotionally to handle a major crisis? In other words, the purpose of crisis management is to teach an organization to confront both the intellectual and emotional stress it will face during the heat of a crisis before it is actually hit by one. It's the purpose of crisis planning to teach an organization how to roll with the punches.

Notice also in Figure 1 that I've only drawn one arrow showing how one set of crises (breaks) can potentially cause another crisis (environmental accidents), for example a Bhopal or a Chernobyl. In reality I could have filled up the entire figure with arrows going every which way, because every crisis is capable of causing and being caused by every other crisis. It certainly is capable of being linked up with every other crisis.

To my colleagues and me, the concept of a crisis portfolio is a sensible way to get any organization thinking beyond tunnel vision or just fighting the last war, that is, merely preparing for the last set of known crises to their industry. For example, no one has to go in and tell the chemical industry to prepare for another Bhopal. Likewise, no one needs to tell the nuclear industry to prepare for another Chernobyl. What needs to be done is to make all organizations realize that potentially they're subject to every one of the families of crises in Figure 1. Instead of taking each crisis literally, we should ask how a Bhopal could happen to us, or better yet, what kind of a Bhopal we could be responsible for either causing or being involved with. Instead of taking product tampering literally—as something that can only happen to Johnson & Johnson—every organization should ask what form of product tampering it is subject to. For instance, go tell the Encyclopedia Britannica people that they weren't involved with product tampering when somebody got into one of their computers and put phony information into it which then got dumped into their encyclopedias. That's product tampering.

Figure 2 shows a similar set of families for the preventive actions organizations can undertake to blunt crises. Here, as well, I recommend the concept of a crisis prevention portfolio. That is, every organization ought to have at least two portfolios, the first one to prepare for the worst in every crisis family that could potentially happen to them, and the second to consider the best out of every preventive action family of what they can do to blunt their crisis potential.

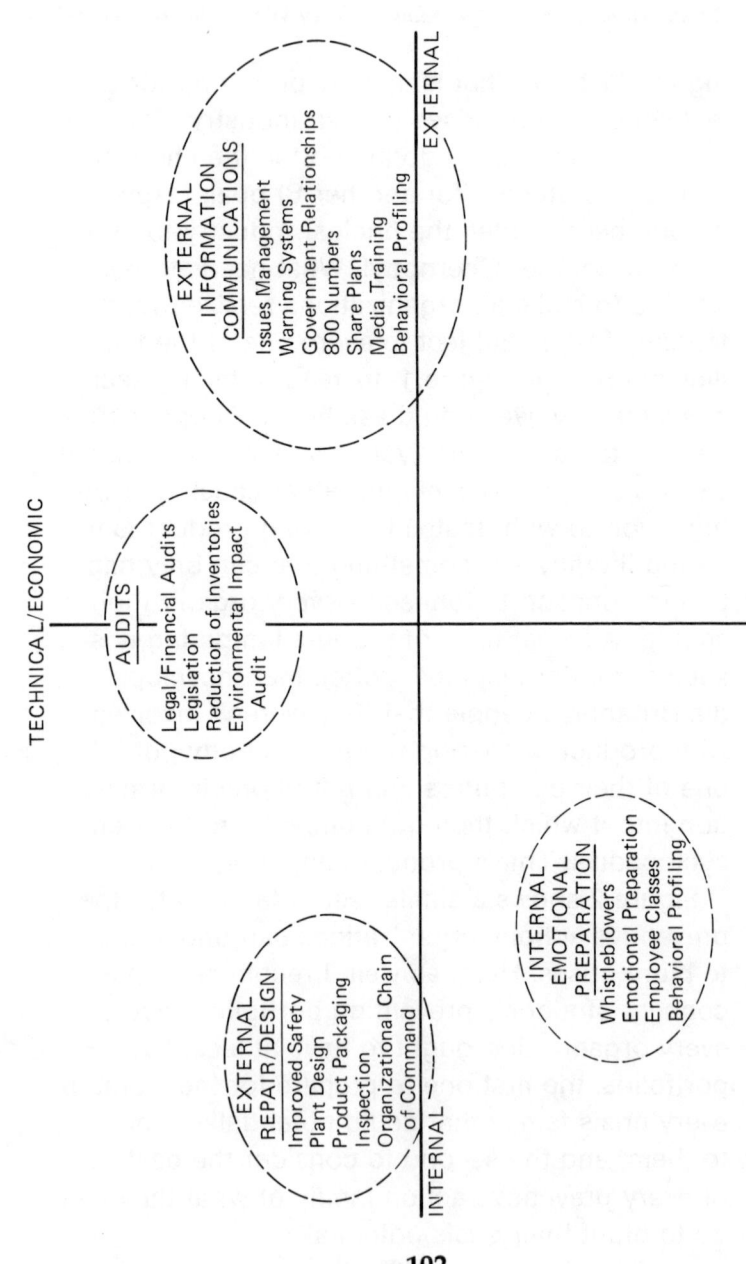

TECHNICAL/ECONOMIC

AUDITS
Legal/Financial Audits
Legislation
Reduction of Inventories
Environmental Impact
Audit

EXTERNAL
INFORMATION
COMMUNICATIONS
Issues Management
Warning Systems
Government Relationships
800 Numbers
Share Plans
Media Training
Behavioral Profiling

EXTERNAL

EXTERNAL
REPAIR/DESIGN
Improved Safety
Plant Design
Product Packaging
Inspection
Organizational Chain
of Command

INTERNAL

INTERNAL
EMOTIONAL
PREPARATION
Whistleblowers
Emotional Preparation
Employee Classes
Behavioral Profiling

PEOPLE/SOCIAL/ORGANIZATIONAL

Let me attempt to seal my case for the concept of dual crisis portfolios by pointing out two striking findings from the study of the *Fortune* 1000 companies. It was found that only thirty-eight percent of the 114 organizations that responded to the survey had crisis management units (CMUs) (by the way, we have reason to believe in the representativeness of the survey results since the list of organizations and industries that responded is highly representative of a broad cross-section of U.S. industries). When the responses of the sample were sorted into two groups, those having a CMU versus those not having a CMU, it was not so surprisingly found that those organizations having a CMU had experienced significantly more crises. Perhaps that's why they set up a CMU in the first place; the majority of respondents agreed that unless an organization had already experienced a major crisis they wouldn't have a serious program of crisis management. However, much more important, it was found that those organizations having a CMU were on the average not only undertaking more preventive actions to blunt crises, but they were also doing more in each of the preventive action families than those organizations not having a CMU. In effect, they had a more balanced crisis portfolio on the prevention side; they were doing more in every one of the crisis prevention families of Figure 2.

TO: Bob

FROM: Steve

DATE: December 16, 1988

SUBJECT: If It Ain't Broke Yet, Now Is the Best Time to Inspect It, Before It Breaks Catastrophically

Let me make some critical observations and points about crisis management in general:

1. Crisis management *is* generic. However distinct different crises appear on the surface, there are nonetheless strong similarities between them. Let me spell out just what this generic character consists of. Every major crisis seems to go through the following key phases (see Figure 1):

   a. Long before its actual occurrence it sends off a repeated and persistent trail of early warning signals announcing its probable occurrence, indicating that if its signals or symptoms are not attended to, then a major crisis will occur. As I said in my last memo, if you have any doubts about this at all, read the *Report of the President's Commission on the Space Shuttle Challenger Accident*. The end of the report is a virtual reproduction—an

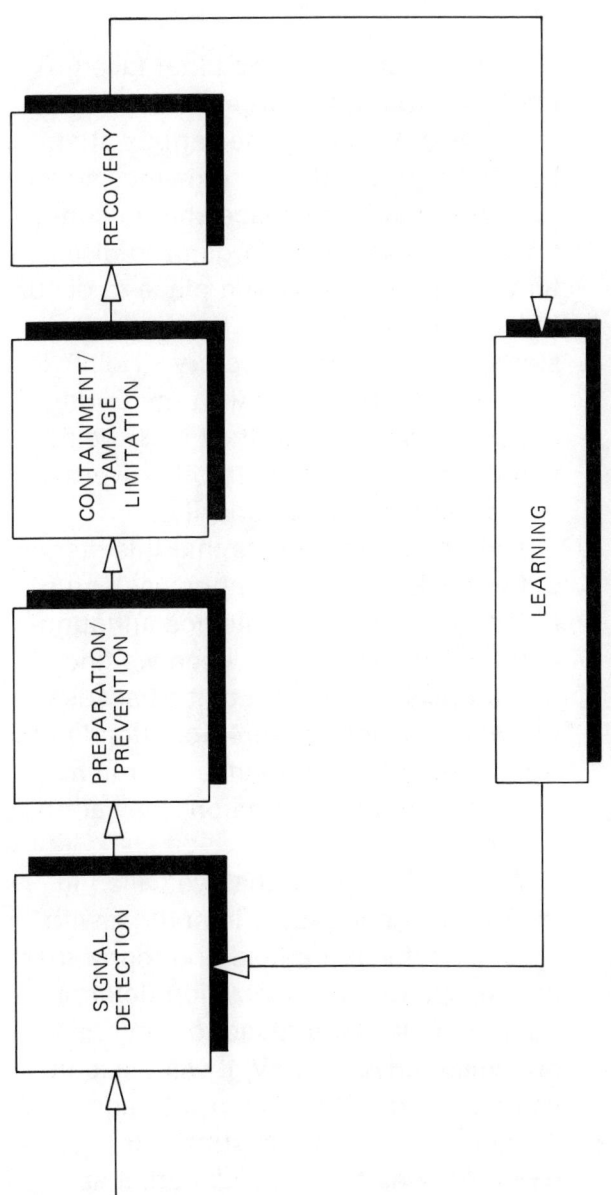

FIGURE 1. The Five Essential Phases of Crisis Management

audit trail—of key memos that failed to make it through the organization to the top of NASA and get the serious attention they deserved. Those memos stated, in effect, that if the space shuttle continued to fly it was an organized disaster looking for a time and place to occur. Indeed, one of the most painful memos starts with the anguished cry, "Help!" It says that the problems with the O-ring are so dangerous that they must be attended to immediately. In other words, they have the highest priority.

The important thing is that this memo did not exist in isolation but was one of a *continuing series* of memos announcing the problem. Often, when we find that a crisis has occurred, it's because the warning signals were not attended to. Again—all crises announce their imminent occurrence long before they actually occur.

The outside group that we called in to advise us conducted interviews with organizations in the field and found that the culture of an organization determines not only how it will respond to a crisis but which crises, if any, it will place in its crisis portfolio to begin with and how it will think about them subsequently. Organizations that they identified as "reactive" persistently and systematically ignore early warning signals, even going so far as to deliberately block them from getting through to management. They do this because their self-image is one of almost complete denial. They have such an inflated self-concept that they see themselves as invulnerable.

Notice how this phase of crisis management links up with the concept of a crisis portfolio. It's important to have different early warning systems in place because the different crises in an organization's crisis portfolio will give off different types of early warning signals. For example, graffiti may be a signal of potential employee disgruntlement while an increasing accident rate may be a symptom of faulty equipment.

b. Organizations need to have *tested, in-place* prevention and preparation mechanisms in order to avert disasters. Notice that I stress "tested, in place." Also notice that this again emphasizes the importance of early warning signals: It's difficult (but not impossible) to prevent that which you haven't detected. You may be able to avert a crisis if you don't have detection systems to pick up its early warning signs, but you're likely to do it as a result of haphazard actions

107

and just plain luck rather than by deliberate intention and design. By God, if doing things by deliberate intention or design is not one of the primary functions of a CEO, then I don't know what is.

The purpose of the prevention and preparation phase is to probe the organization actively for every sign of weakness and potential breakdown before a determined external adversary like a saboteur, assassin, or terrorist can and to try to do everything possible to lessen the chances of breakdown. The guiding principle is: "If it ain't broke, that's the time to make sure that it stays fixed by continually probing for inherent weaknesses." I believe a cardinal rule of crisis management ought to be the following: Any employee, but especially a top executive, ought to be fired immediately and automatically if he or she utters the cliche, "If it ain't broke, don't fix it." This cliche may apply to many aspects of a business, but the one area in which it surely doesn't apply is crisis management. Anybody with the "don't fix it" attitude is part of the problem and not part of the solution.

By the way, it should be pointed out that no one in the field of crisis management says that we'll ever be perfect. Indeed, complete or perfect prevention of

all crises is not the point of crisis planning or crisis management at all. It's anal-
ogous to protecting your house from a
burglar. Even though we know we can't
keep all burglars out, that doesn't mean
we ought not to try to make it as difficult
as possible by putting in deterrents.

c. The next phase of crisis management is
having *tested, in-place* damage limitation
mechanisms. Since we can't prevent all
crises, the purpose of these mechanisms
is to prevent the damage from spreading
and engulfing other parts of the corporation. A good metaphor might be to keep
the fire or the oil spill from spreading
and contaminating unwanted areas. Once
NASA's catastrophic explosion occurred
in front of millions of people, it was virtually impossible to keep the damage from
spreading; indeed, it threatened to engulf
the whole organization and place the very
existence of the space program in doubt.

d. The next phase is having *tested, in-place,*
short-term and long-term recovery mechanisms. Notice that I'm constantly stressing "tested, in place" because the one
thing we know is that under the stress
and heat of a crisis, it is very difficult to
invent these things on the spot. In fact,
that's what really is so reactive about re-

109

active management. If you're not antici-
patory then you are forced into reacting,
that is, inventing and patching things up
after the fact.

e. The last phase is continued learning and
reassessment to improve what you've
done in the past.

2. To argue that you don't need a permanent
crisis management team is to assume that
your organization is better than the FBI.

Bob, I have to tell you an experience I
had recently. It was most illuminating. I had
the opportunity to visit the FBI Academy in
Quantico, Virginia, and to talk to a special
agent there who works in the field of crisis
management. He works mainly with police
departments around the country. His job is
to try to educate them to the fact that whenever they're faced with a dangerous situation like a hostage or terrorist action, they
ought to consider a whole range of possible
actions instead of just directly using force
to try to free hostages. His point is that in
some cases it might be more effective to
try to talk a terrorist or hostage taker out of
the situation than to act through sheer force
alone.

During the course of the conversation,
something fascinating came out. The major
assumption that he makes as an FBI agent

is that whenever there is a *persistent* and *repeated* threat to life, limb, or property, one needs a *specially trained* unit to deal with that threat. Notice the key words "persistent" and "repeated." Also notice the key phrase "specially trained." The point is that all crises exact not only a severe financial toll on an organization but also a severe emotional toll. For instance, I heard that during the height of the Challenger disaster, NASA had to set up emergency medical hotlines for their employees. In a number of cases, NASA employees were faced by this "seemingly innocent question" from their children: "Mommy, Daddy, were you responsible for killing the astronauts?" If we think that ordinary people can handle such questions, or the stress of a catastrophic accident they may have strong guilt feelings about, we're dead wrong. They can't handle such stress without special training.

From what I heard, much of the stress surrounding the explosion was transferred not only to NASA employees but to their spouses and children as well. The point is that you need both special *intellectual* training to know how to think through crisis situations and a lot of *emotional* preparation in order to handle them as well. Reactive organizations are just not sensitive to this; that's one reason they get into trouble. Notice again that a critical assumption is being made. If you and your organization don't think that you need a specially trained crisis management unit, in effect the assumption you're making is, "We're better than the FBI." That's a hell of a strong assumption to make in today's world. At the very least we ought to be aware when we are making such an assumption.

3. Bob, of all the problems I know of, crisis management is one of the most interdisciplinary. I think modern crises now crisscross not only whole industries but every conceivable functional specialty within our organization. The thing I have observed is that different parts of an organization tend to own different crises. One part will be most susceptible to terrorism, another to product tampering, another to faulty communications, and the like. The trouble is that often these different parts don't get together and realize how, even in the case of the crises I've just mentioned, they can link up and cause a crisis in more than one part of the organization simultaneously. A terrorist action in one part can lead to misinformation or product tampering in another part of an organization.

The point is that you need somebody somewhere to coordinate all of this. In fact the argument that I've been making goes to one of the deepest parts of how reactive organizations respond to crises, namely that a system is no more than the sum of its separate parts. I take sharp issue with this. For me a system is the *product* of the interactions among its parts. It's the product of how all its parts multiply, interact with one another, and thus intensify their actions. This leads to my next counter-assumption.

4. It's important to realize that crises can result from a variety of causes and conditions, not a specific set. It may have been true in the past that a very specific set of conditions was both necessary and sufficient to cause a particular crisis. But I don't believe that happens in today's world. You mean to tell me that there's one and only one way for a Chernobyl to happen; one and only one way for a Bhopal to happen; one and only one way for a massive incident of product tampering to happen? I just don't believe it.

5. *I'm not talking fundamentally about crisis management in this memo or in all my memos to you. Everything I've said is equally applicable to every issue with which we have to deal.* If you take a look at the basic model of crisis management (see Figure 1)—picking up early warning signals, preparing for and trying to prevent major crises, limiting the damage, engaging in short-term and long-term recovery—with

just a very small change in wording, this same general model applies to everyday business decisions as well. Don't you and I as CEOs have to pick up and monitor very carefully not only signals of what the opposition or competition is doing, but also new opportunities in the marketplace as well? Don't we have to prepare our organizations for taking advantage of these opportunities? Instead of damage limitation and recovery mechanisms, don't we have to institute formal change procedures to get our organizations to adapt to new conditions? (Recall our first memos about change?)

Here are two of the most important assumptions that underlie this whole discussion:

Organizations don't create the crises they face; crises just happen.	Organizations do create the crises they face in the special sense that the kinds of early warning systems, prevention, damage limitation, recovery, and learning mechanisms they institute are one of the most important factors affecting what kinds of crises result.

If "doing nothing" and "doing what we've always done in the past" are not attitudes that create crises, then I don't know what are.

From Star Wars
to Economic Wars

TO: Bob Fountain

FROM: Steve Hart

DATE: March 4, 1989

SUBJECT: From Stars Wars to Economic Wars

I've been trying your process of examining assumptions, slowly at first, and then on bigger and bigger issues. I even involved some of my key people in learning it by doing it. The brightest, of course, took to it right away. By brightest, I don't mean just those with more analytic smarts, e.g., our scientists and engineers, but those with intuitive smarts, those who can grasp the big issues.

One of the brightest guys in our organization, believe it or not, is a young computer scientist named Gary Bond. He's not only got the analytical skills to run our computer operations, but he's just naturally intuitive. I think he intuitively understands what Albert Einstein said a long time ago, "Imagination is more important than knowledge." What he's been doing is looking at the complexities involved in the writing of the huge computer programs that will be needed to run President Reagan's Star Wars Initiative (SDI). (As you know, some of our work is defense-related.) What he found is that the whole issue is so plagued with paradoxes it casts extreme doubt on the whole Star Wars program; however, something far more interesting came out.

Through the study of *one* messy global phenomenon—the conduct of nuclear war, or better yet, its supposed prevention through Star Wars—all of us began to see that the paradoxes that Gary uncovered were also applicable to the new global economy. As a result, we've developed some even better insights as to what's different about today's environment and how to manage better within it. Indeed, I believe this understanding has given our firm a real advantage in starting some new businesses that take advantage of this complexity.

We've found, in fact, that a whole new range of products and services is perfectly suited to the new environment. Briefly, they are products and services that integrate a lot of separate features so that they help our clients get a handle on complexity. In other words, we found a whole new set of businesses that are directed toward helping people deal with the complexity in their lives. Customers are willing to pay quite handsomely for anything that promises to do away with some of the fragmentation in their lives. So we do the integration for them and then sell it back to them at a quite reasonable but still handsome profit.

Once you reach the level of the whole globe, where potentially everything can interact with everything else, weird effects begin to show up. In a word, actions that are good in isolation can have reverse, completely counterintuitive effects when magnified to the level of the whole globe. But let me give you the background to make this clear. Let me trace the steps by which Gary reached his conclusions.

Almost from the day of their invention, it was realized that paradoxes of all kinds arose in thinking through various strategies and options for using nuclear weapons. For instance, early on in their history it was realized that given their vast destructive power, the only valid purpose for the existence of nuclear weapons was to *prevent* their being used by either side. Thus, *nuclear weapons existed in order to serve the purpose of not being used,* for their actual use would literally spell an end to human existence. Putting it another way, if both sides felt "equally insecure" because of their ability to deliver a lethal blow, then presumably both would feel "secure." Thus, mutual *in*security presumably guaranteed mutual security because both sides would be restrained from striking one another. The notion of paradox attendant to nuclear weapons is nothing new.

What Gary found that *is* new is that there was not a single aspect of nuclear strategy that did not have a significant paradox associated with it. So the extent to which such strategies are affected by paradox is much deeper and greater

119

than I think we've realized previously. As a result, *the management of nuclear strategy is equivalent to the management of paradox.*

What I'm going to try to do is to lead you to the conclusion that, by implication, *the management of paradox is also absolutely critical to the management of the global economy and indeed to all phenomena which are global.* Let's work toward this by considering Star Wars.

The first point to realize is that Star Wars will, it is estimated, require a computer program roughly 10 to 100 times bigger than anything that has been written thus far, or approximately 10 to 100 million lines of computer instructions. The program needed is so big because it is required to perform the innumerable calculations necessary to make the decision as to which enemy missiles to shoot down during which point in their flight paths, thereby presumably making us more secure through a greater defensive capability rather than through a greater offensive capability.

Now Bob, you and I both know that it is virtually impossible to write a computer program, no matter how short it is, that will work perfectly the first time. Imagine then the "bugs" or imperfections in a program as huge as 10 to 100 million lines! Here's precisely where paradox enters in.

One way to test the effectiveness of the computer program for Star Wars is to send up a wave of our own missiles whose trajectories we know precisely. (At some point we have to test the program against actual missiles; otherwise, we'd be dependent on another computer program to test the first one, and then we'd have to have supreme confidence in the second one to validate the first one, etc., etc., etc.) Hence, we can then test the effectiveness of the program by shooting down the missiles. However, to really test the program to its limits we'd have to send up a *sizable swarm* of missiles because that's presumably what the *USSR* would do during a real strike.

Query: How do we assure the Russians that the test swarm is only a simulation and not a first strike directed toward them? In order for them to go along with us, they would have to trust us, the very quality that has been missing to begin with or we would not have been able to get Star Wars through our political system. Hence, the paradox: The less trust there is between us and our adversaries, the more we build weapons of bigger scope (whether they are defensive or offensive); as a consequence, however, such weapons are more complex and require more extensive test procedures, but such procedures necessitate greater end (i.e., more) trust and cooperation between us and our adversaries in order to carry out the test. But then why should they cooperate with us to further a weapon that is presumably to their disadvantage? (Notice also that this discussion makes clear why on the scale of global issues the whole distinction between "defensive" and "offensive" weapons collapses; it's no longer a viable distinction at this level; it's much the same as the irrelevance of "objective" and "subjective" or "hard" and "soft" that we were talking about in one of our previous memos.)

The attempt to secure a decisive advantage or security through technology alone is self-defeating because the testing of the resultant technology depends upon trust and cooperation from the adversary, the very things that were missing in the first place and thus prompted the building of the technology! But if such trust and cooperation are missing initially, where and how do they magically appear subsequently, especially, God forbid, in the heat of war, an extreme state that does not exactly contribute to the building of additional trust. No one has been able to answer this key question satisfactorily.

Gary's extensive study of the propositions and paradoxes connected with nuclear strategy revealed that they fall into four principal categories or classes:

1. More is or leads to more; i.e., "bigger is better."
2. Less is or leads to less; i.e., "weakness leads to weakness."
3. More is or leads to less; i.e., "not only is bigger not better, but it leads to its direct opposite."

4. Less is or leads to more; i.e., "small is beautiful or small is better."

   Star Wars is a prime illustration of "more leads to less," i.e., more of something initially thought to be desirable (a greater defensive shield which presumably precludes having to trust the adversary) leads to secondary effects or end results counter to the original proposed benefits (the resultant computer program needed to run a Star Wars is so complex that it requires even greater end trust from the adversary, but greater trust is precluded by the whole process itself). Thus, a greater defensive shield may leave us worse off in the end, whether it works or not, because it may decrease even further the already low state of trust between us.
   However, there is something deeper about Star Wars that shows even more dearly just what kind of a nutty world we've now entered. Star Wars, like all global phenomena, actually falls into every one of the above four categories of reasoning *simultaneously*. The phenomenon is so complex that it literally has significant aspects that fit into all four categories at once. Thus in the case of Star Wars the following four propositions are *all plausible* to varying degrees at the same time:

1. "More leads to more": A bigger defensive shield does "promise" the U.S. the end benefit of more security; it also promises to force the USSR to the bargaining table, i.e., a greater end-benefit.

2. "Less leads to less": Less trust breeds bigger or more weapons which in turn breed less trust.

3. "More leads to less": Bigger weapons breed even less trust and/or less felt security; in addition, "more leads to more" in (1) above may backfire and thus lead to less, for while (1) may restrain the USSR and force it to the bargaining table, there may be a greater chance of an error due to the breakdown of a more complex system. The result would be a lesser end state for all parties.

4. "Less leads to more": Fewer weapons may promise more felt security because they may not threaten the other side as much. The opposite side of the argument is that fewer weapons may actually encourage the other side to be more aggressive, thus cycling the whole series of propositions back to (1).

Once we reached the preceding realizations, we didn't stop there. When we had the basic pattern that revealed itself through Gary's study of nuclear strategy, we began to see that it popped out all over the place. It didn't apply just to nuclear weapons. It applied to the new global economic situation as well. By now, I could give you literally hundreds of examples, but let me present just a few.

Consider one which reveals unambiguously not only the general industrial strategy the Japanese have pursued but the specific senses of "more leads to more" and "less leads to less" that they have adopted. The example also demonstrates the applicability of what we have been discussing to the arena of industrial or competitive strategy:

> [Japanese companies] are often criticized by their Western counterparts for their obsession with market share. But in a growing market, competitive position and the rate at which that position is changing are the most important indices of performance. Increased market share and increased competitive advantage is obtained by preempting market growth with aggressive pricing and investment policies [i.e., this is the specific sense in which the Japanese have defined "more leads to more," or "greater aggressiveness leads to greater market share"]. A noncompetitive [i.e., "less"] pricing policy and/or the failure to add sufficient plant and equipment capacity and human resources will result in a loss of competitive position [i.e., "less leads to less"]. If a competitive position is allowed to deteriorate substantially the viability of the business will ultimately be threatened ["less will lead to less"]. (J.C. Abegglen & G. Stalk, Jr., *Kaisha, The Japanese Corporation.* New York: Basic Books, 1985, p. 45)

The Japanese have also combined these with a "less is more" principle by "focusing" their energies in niche markets, thus showing that it is the *total* combination of principles or categories

125

that is important for an integrated strategy in the global or world economy.

Let me give you another example. Recently there was an article in *Business Week* entitled "Is Deregulation Working?". The point of the article was that deregulation, that is the breaking down of government regulations that were supposed to protect certain industries from competitive practices, supposedly to lead to greater productivity and competition by strengthening the concept of the free market, has actually had just the reverse effect. The example is a perfect illustration of how instead of "more leading to more"—i.e., more deregulation, supposedly a good thing leading to an even better operation of the free market—it has had just the reverse effect. It's a perfect example of how more can lead to less if you don't understand the whole system in which anything functions. *Unless the complexities of the whole system are taken into account, something which in isolation appears good can have the opposite of intended effects.*

The reason why more or greater deregulation didn't work the way it was supposed to is as follows. One of the chief goals of deregulation was to break up the cozy cartels that supposedly flourished under regulation. Breaking these cartels down would supposedly introduce new competitors into markets. In the beginning, that's what took place. In the end, however, the power of the big, established players derived largely from their extensive networks of transportation and telecommunications facilities.

If anything, these networks have expanded even more under deregulation by acquiring and linking up with smaller players. What happened is that the people who fashioned the deregulation movement vastly underestimated how much these huge networks served as entry barriers to prevent others from getting into the game. To quote from *Business Week,* "Network owners enjoyed economies of flow or density, which are similar to the more familiar economies of scale in that average costs decline as network traffic increases. This gives the owner of a large network a clear cost advantage over a small network owner—and enormous market clout" (*Business Week,* December 22, 1986. Reprinted by permission.)

I keep repeating myself, but again the point is you have to take account of the whole system in fashioning any strategy.

TO: Bob

FROM: Steve

DATE: April 5, 1989

SUBJECT: Development, Not Growth:
Less Is More

Let me explore even further with you what I laid out in my last memo.

In 1946, Albert Einstein saw clearly that the invention of nuclear weapons had ushered in the most profound change in human affairs in all of history. At the heart of his concern was the deep fear that our basic ways of thinking had not kept pace with the revolution that nuclear weapons had effected. Einstein expressed his concern in a famous and oft quoted statement: "The unleashed power of the atom has changed everything save our modes of thinking and thus we drift towards unparalleled catastrophe."

The simple relationship "more leads to more" that I talked about in my last memo has been the normal order of things, or "business as usual," up to recent times. In fact, the twin complementary patterns of reasoning, "more is more" and "less is less" are the primary patterns that have governed our thinking about war and most phenomena in our civilization for so long.

The first one is the old familiar line, "bigger is better." The second one is just as familiar: "Weakness leads to weakness."

It's not hard to understand how both these patterns applied in simpler times. If you had ten archers and I had only five, then all other things being equal, your ten were superior to my five. For even if I knocked out five of your archers, you'd still have five left to threaten me with retaliation.

Global phenomena, which nuclear weapons represent, have clearly changed all of this. It's no longer clear that the side with greater weapons is ahead once both sides reach levels of armaments that are lethal. In effect, you reach a boomerang point. At a certain point, more or greater numbers of anything does not lead to more security. Rather, it leads to just the reverse.

The pattern "more leads to less" represents the breakdown of the pattern "bigger is better" that has governed our civilization for so long. It represents nothing less than the shift from the pattern of thinking that was appropriate for the world conceived in the image of a machine, that is, the world ushered in by the Industrial Revolution, to the pattern that is now appropriate for a world that is one big, complex, intertwined system. For the world that functioned as a machine, the principle "bigger is better" was appropriate. Bigger inputs into the machine (more resources, money, etc.) did lead to bigger desirable outputs (more products, greater productivity, higher quality of life, etc.).

Increasingly we find the exact reverse on every front and level of society. If this is indeed the case, then a clear understanding of the new patterns that underlie all global phenomena may be the most critical task facing contemporary civilization if we are to survive in every facet of our existence. That's why the work that Gary Bond did for us is so significant. It begins to make clear what those patterns are.

Once you've become sensitized to the pattern "more leads to less" you can see it pop out all over the place. Consider a few examples that I came across a few years ago:

> To reduce domestic hunger we grow more food, which requires greater use of energy for farm equipment, fertilizers, and transportation, adding to the price of energy, which raises the cost of food, putting it out of the price range of the needy [i.e., growing more food leads to its lesser availability to the poor].
>
> To solve the problem of soaring crime rates, cities expand the law enforcement establishment, which draws funds away from other services such as schools, welfare, and job training, which leads to more poverty, addiction, prostitution, and more crime.
>
> To ward off coronary heart disease, people who live in cities spend more time jogging and cycling, which exposes their lungs to more air pollution than normal, increasing the risk of coronary illness.

To ease traffic congestion, multi-lane highways are built, which draws people away from mass transit so that the new road soon becomes as overcrowded as the old road.

To reduce energy use and pollution, cities invest in mass transit, which raises municipal debt, leading to a reduction in frequency and quality of service and an increase in fares, which reduces ridership, which further raises the municipal debt. (Karl E. Weick, "Small Wins, Redefining the Scale of Social Problems," *American Psychologist,* January 1984, p. 40)

As a culture, we've been so hooked on the notion that "bigger is better" that we still believe that on every front we can *grow* our way out of all our problems. As a result, we have yet to appreciate the differences between "growth" and "development" and the notion that in order to meet our problems, we now need to develop, not grow.

Growth is the natural accompaniment of "bigger is better." It is typically measured in quantitative terms. Thus, if a firm had a ten percent ROI, or return on its corporate investment, last year, then under a growth model, its goal is to do fifteen percent or twenty percent ROI next quarter, next year, etc.

Development, on the other hand is measured qualitatively. It is the epitome of what I call "less can be more." Its goal is to develop the *quality* of working life of its members so that together they can produce quality products to compete internationally. I know of no more powerful way of summarizing the differences between the two than by quoting Russell Ackoff, one of this country's leading strategic thinkers: *"Cemeteries grow each year but they don't develop."* That's precisely what's been the trouble with some of our dinosaur industries. They've grown ponderously in size without developing their brains and their hearts. As an article in *Business Week* put it:

> Even if [Roger] Smith [GM's CEO] can solve his company's myriad other ailments, he faces that day of reckoning with one thing that is GM's very essence: *its size* [my emphasis]. The basic question nagging this biggest, most diverse, and most integrated of car companies is whether it is *just too big* to compete in today's fast changing car market [my emphasis]. Given GM's history, its apparent inability to live off of fewer cars is not surprising. But it is expensive. The turn-arounds at Ford and Chrysler largely reflect decisions to scale back capacity, so that they can break even with lower production levels. GM's break even point has risen 30% since 1981. (*Business Week,* March 16, 1987, p. 110. Reprinted by permission.)

Let me close by contrasting two opposing sets of assumptions which get at what I was trying to express in my last memo.

Old Operating Assumptions

1. Bigger is always better, i.e., we can continue increasing the scale of all operations indefinitely and by so doing reap bigger and bigger rewards.

2. We can assess the benefits of anything without having to know its effects on the whole or larger system.

3. We can grow our way out of any problems we face.

New Operating Assumptions

1. Less is now more; bigger is only better if we understand its effects on the whole system.

2. To repeat: The only sense in which bigger is better is if we can understand its effects on the whole system of which anything is but a part. We cannot get by without knowing the effects of any of our proposed actions on the whole system.

3. We can handle our problems only if we learn to develop with regard to them.

Going Against the Grain of U.S. Culture in Order to Compete Internationally

TO: Steve

FROM: Bob

DATE: June 1, 1989

SUBJECT: Going Against the Grain of
American Culture

What a struggle this past year has been. But how much we've learned. I think we've both got our money's worth on the intellectual investment we've made. It has been a great game of Ping-Pong.

As a result of our conversations, plus my beginning to understand what's so different about today's environment, I've begun to see that if America is to be truly competitive in international markets, then we're going to have to reevaluate not just our detailed business practices, but also some of the basic values that underlie our culture. In other words, I've seen that there is more to understanding people than psychology alone can provide. You also need to understand a lot of things like anthropology if you're going to account for the values of a culture as a whole.

As a result of reading a lot of books, attending lectures, etc., I think I've identified sixteen core values that underlie our culture. To be sure, there are more than just sixteen things that make us distinct as a people. But I think that each of these

sixteen plays a vital role in our ability, or rather
our inability, to compete globally. What I've been
trying to do in my company is to go against the
grain of these values while at the same time not
totally denying them because there is much in
them that I still believe in as well. In effect, I've
been using the change chart that I presented in
one of my earliest memos to think through the
issue and chart our company's strategy. It's not
hard to see that most of the things we need to
do fall, to differing degrees, in the difficult-but-
necessary-to-change quadrant. The values I have
identified are:

1. *Our cultural rank or standing: We believe
   we're God's chosen people. We're number
   one.* Steve, if you read the earliest accounts
   of the founding of this country, it's clear
   that when the Pilgrims were making their
   journey to America they conceived of the
   new land that they were coming to in mys-
   tical, religious terms. They probably had
   to do this in order to fortify themselves for
   the difficult journey they were undertaking. Only God really knew what they were
   getting into. They conceived of America
   as a holy shrine, standing high on a hill or
   holy mountain. This was perhaps appropriate for the time, but it imbued in Americans
   the notion that they were truly anointed by
   God to settle this new land and occupy a

privileged place in the universe. As a result, everybody else was inferior. In effect, we were morally superior and thus fit to lead the world.

Don't misconstrue me. To say that I no longer believe that we're God's chosen people does not mean that we have to accept an inferior status. It just means that we can no longer be so arrogant as to believe that we're the world's standard, because once you start believing that, then you end up believing that you can't learn anything from anybody else. It's not a good attitude to proceed from if you want to sell your goods to the rest of the world. You've got to make yourself as well as those you're trying to sell to feel that we're equal partners. In fact, isn't the point that the economies of the world are now so intertwined that we're all in the same boat anyway? If one of the major economies crashes, don't they all?

No longer believing that you're God's chosen people doesn't mean that you're accepting second place; it just means that your esteem, how you feel about yourself, isn't dependent on being number one.

2. *Revered heroes/gods: Celebrities.* We're too hooked on celebrities as gods in our society. I believe this is wrong because it devalues the serious work undertaken by

artists, scientists, musicians, and engineers. In America today, the attitude is almost "If you're not a celebrity you're nothing." The worst of it is that the people we revere are so superficial that the values they espouse are not enough to get us through in the long haul. To make it in the long haul, you've got to know something; you've got to have some depth.

A book by Neil Postman, *Amusing Ourselves to Death,* makes the point that for the most part in America today, Americans no longer engage in serious conversation; they entertain one another. I believe this attitude has affected so much of what we do that we're no longer interested in serious content. We're interested in amusing ourselves, cheap entertainment. How can we produce anything of lasting value if that's our attitude? This doesn't mean we have to walk around with a serious, sour face all the time; it just means putting things in proper perspective.

In my organization, I'm insistent about our not using fads to guide our thinking about where we want to go and to be as a company. I'll be damned if I'll let somebody dictate our values without any challenge.

3. *Magnitude of efforts sought/scale of activities.* In every case strength is preferred; our culture generally believes in *overwhelming*

any problem. Bigger is better, subtlety is neither generally preferred nor encouraged, and high technology is preferred to simple technology. I don't think I have to say more about this one since we've pursued it throughout our discussions. The bottom line is that we no longer follow bigger is better as a knee-jerk response. We attempt to think through as carefully as we can the magnitude of effort every problem requires.

4. *Social measuring rod or ruler.* Quantitative measures are almost always preferred to qualitative measures; this results from our prolonged history of British empiricism, from which much of our culture's philosophy is derived. The notion is, "If you can put a number on it, then and only then is it real and important." I don't think I need to say much about this given your, and now my, emphasis on assumptions which are quintessentially qualitative. Quality and quantity go hand in hand; they can't be separated, as our very first memos to one another still demonstrate.

5. *Time horizons: The immediate here and now.* The future is almost entirely discounted; there is an extreme discounting of future generations. Our time horizon for planning is extremely short, if not non-existent.

6. *Preferred form of social organization: Bureaucracy.*

7. *Attitude toward government: Distrust.* Unlike the Japanese, who view theirs as an ally, ours is viewed as the enemy.

8. *Ultimate unit of social reality: The individual.* As a result, we experience extreme social and personal fragmentation as the traditional social binding mechanisms such as the family and religion have virtually collapsed.

9. *Memory: History, tradition, continuity.* These have almost vanished.

10. *Attitude toward evil: Almost complete denial and unawareness that evil is part of every human being and society.* As a result, we either *over-* or *under*-evaluate others; thus, for instance, we tend either to project all evil onto our adversaries such as the Russians, calling them the Evil Empire, or, in the recent case of Iran, we tend to underestimate them. We fail to see that they "are not like us," and hence in a case where it was important to view the adversary as having *some* degree of evil, we failed to do so.

11. *Attitude toward education: Inferior/show business.* This results almost as the trivialization of American society.

12. *Epistemology, the way systems are organized: Machine-like, hierarchical, reductionistic.* This means we still believe that when something breaks, the broken part can simply be lifted out of the simple machine of which it is a part, and a new part can be inserted. We fail to comprehend that the broken or defective aspects of complex systems no longer have simple or sole causes.

13. *Relationship of technology and people.* In almost all cases faith is placed in technology versus people.

14. *What other people would choose to be/the standard/the model.* The assumption here is that everyone, if given a choice, would choose to be American, would aspire to be like us, that essentially, they love us. Again, the U.S. is the world standard.

15. *Essential differences.* The assumption here is that everybody everywhere is essentially the same; thus even though we are number one, the world is still basically homogeneous; people are only lesser degrees of inferior models of us or at lower or lesser stages of their development.

16. *Isolation or relationship to the rest of the world: Parochial.* For instance, we don't need to learn the language or the customs of the countries in which we want to do business.

As I've said, we have found it necessary to go against every one of these values if we are to compete. Let me give you just one example. To counteract the effects of bureaucracy and individualism, we've experimented with having our top executives, including me, share offices. In this way, we can constantly share the information we need in order to make quick, integrated decisions. It simply takes too long for the right information to flow up, down, and across channels, walls, and departments in the traditional bureaucracies. No wonder they can't adapt and shift quickly. Their structure gets in the way. Or better yet, the values and assumptions which underlie their structure are killing them.

I thought you'd enjoy the following, which shows how other cultures organize themselves differently because of their values:

> Given the advantages of their system, it hardly seems surprising that the Japanese are more comfortable doing business with familiar suppliers. But U.S. parts manufacturers are learning that they can win business if they adapt to Japanese ways. Globe Industries, a maker of sound control and acoustical equipment in Chicago, has been selling sound absorbing materials to Honda since 1980. "The Japanese aren't buying the part, they're buying the company," says Matthew Smith, Globe's Marketing Vice President. "Every U.S. supplier that wants to do business with them must learn to be *less independent* [my emphasis] than he has been in the past." Globe has to disclose many of its costs to Honda and allow frequent inspections of its plants.

But the loss of independence brings rewards [my emphasis]: The Japanese can be immensely helpful. "We'll move moats to protect our suppliers in financial trouble," says Runyon of Nissan. When Globe had to modify a part it sells to Honda, Smith says, the Honda people immediately formed a joint task force to help. "The tendency with GM and Ford in such cases is finger pointing," says Smith. "They say, 'you screwed up,' which forces us to react defensively. While we may solve the problem eventually, it's after a lot more heart beating and perspiration."

Much of the apparent discrimination, in short, appears to be not against American companies because they are American, but because they are poor performers. If U.S. suppliers only stew about prejudice, real or imagined, they will be foregoing the one chance they have to solve their problems. "We put our brainpower and development senses on hold for a few years, and the Japanese went right by us. . . . Now we've got to regain our competitiveness." What the suppliers see as a conspiracy, Japanese customers—and increasingly their American counterparts—see as common business sense: They want to buy from the company that can do the best job. (Edward Boyer, "Are Japanese Managers Biased Against Americans?" *Fortune,* September 1, 1986, pp. 74–75. Reprinted by permission from *Fortune* magazine; © 1986 Time Inc. All rights reserved.)

Steve, a closing note. I guess I've finally learned what I only knew abstractly before: It takes real pain in order to change. And even this isn't enough since a lot of us are in pain a great deal of the time. If what we've had to go through is typical, then I'm afraid only the toughest will change. You've got to really want it to make it through the anxiety. Anyone who minimizes the anxiety connected with significant change is a fool—maybe, stronger yet, evil.

I once heard someone say that all people suffer up to the full level of their capacity or ability. If that's so, then maybe, paradoxically, we have to increase our ability to feel pain, to suffer, if we are really going to change.

TO: Steve

FROM: Bob

DATE: July 7, 1989

SUBJECT:

I recently reread an article from *Foreign Affairs.* It summarizes everything we've said. It's so important that I give you a rather long quote:

> Throughout the world the problems of sluggish growth, financial instability, Third World debt and trade imbalances are interlocked—and lie at the heart of America's problems. As Nobel Laureate Lawrence R. Klein has put it, both the U.S. budget and trade deficits and the related problems of sluggish growth, overcapacity and unemployment are "endogenous" to the world economic system. It now appears that these problems cannot be solved by the United States alone but must be solved within the context of that wider system.
>   What do these new conditions and dangers imply for economic policy? *The greatest change required appears to be that the unit for policy thinking must become the world economy rather than the national economy, although this flies in the face of traditional national politics and economic pressures* [my emphasis]. National policy makers must be concerned with the wider community of interests, thinking not only about conflicts with adversaries but about mutually supportive relations with allies and trading partners as well. Whether or not

the current U.S. Administration is able to tackle the problems facing the world economy, the challenge is of such magnitude that it will be with us for some years.

. . . *In sum, there are no "technical" solutions to the economic problems the world is facing* [my emphasis]. What is most needed is political will—the will of the United States to deal more effectively with its own problems and the will of all the major industrial countries to work together for a common end. It is easy enough to say that, with the lessening of American dominance and a diffusion of economic power, Japan and Germany must accept wider international responsibilities and join the United States in efforts to prevent a crackup after the greatest period of growth the world economy has ever experienced. (Leonard Silk, "The United States and the World Economy," *Foreign Affairs,* Vol. 65, No. 3, 1987, pp. 458–476. Reprinted by permission.)

This says it all, doesn't it?

So we come down to perhaps two of the most important assumptions that need to be contrasted. The assumption on the left is the one that applied to the world economy for so long; the assumption on the right is the one that is now operative:

1. If the economy of one of the major powers fails, it does not necessarily lead to the failure of the others. In other words, the assumption is that the economies of the world are essentially independent even though of course they can strongly influence one another.

1. The world economies are interdependent. If any one of the economies of the major powers fails, it is very likely, indeed more than likely, that all of them will fail; if they don't fail then they will be so strongly affected as to experience a major turn, a direction from which they may not recover.

I've invested so much time in educating you, I'd like to draw upon you. I have some new problems with which I now need *your* help. I'll be getting back to you soon with some more memos.

Take care!

MEMO 18

The Parable of the Oil Company: Paradigm Shift

TO: Bob

FROM: Steve

DATE: July 21, 1989

SUBJECT: It's Time to Shift Paradigms

If you think I'm going to let you have the last
word on this go-round between us, you're crazy.
Indeed, there won't ever be any last word between us.

I'd like to share with you something that I
picked up at a talk I attended recently. There
are so many of these things coming at us so fast,
each one summarizing what's so different about
today's world, that we can just go and on producing examples, but I think you'll find this one
particularly interesting.

Recently, I listened to an analyst who was an
expert on the oil industry. What he presented
was so absolutely fundamental and central that I
believe it describes what *all* businesses are going
through today.

Take a look at Figure 1. It's my reproduction and summary of one of the slides that the
speaker was using. The three curves at the lower
left of the figure represent how the oil company
invested in research and development on different fossil fuels over a period of time to develop them as businesses. The first curve, which

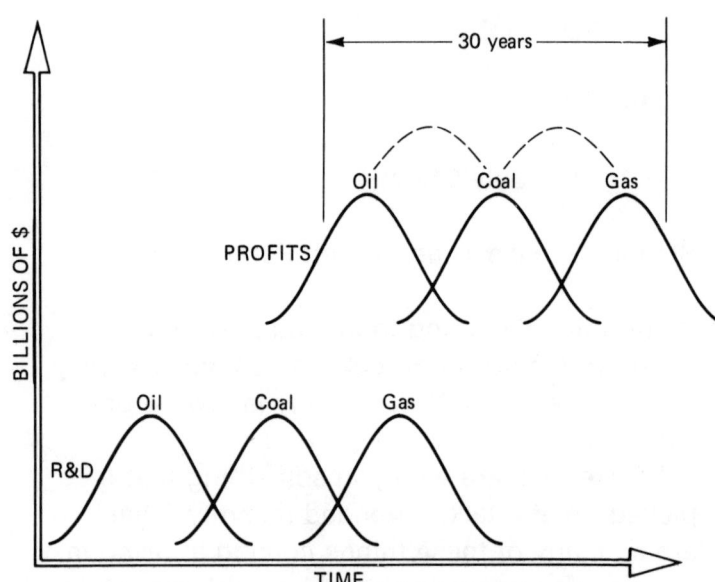

FIGURE 1. R & D Profits Over Time

pertains to oil, shows that initially the company
pumped a lot of money not only into exploring
for new oil fields, but also into developing refiner-
ies as a business so they could produce gasoline
and oil products at the other end. You can see
that this is a kind of normal-shaped curve that
applies pretty much to the development of any
business. You put in a lot of money in the beginning to develop new products and then your
investment in R&D tails off as the business becomes mature.

Notice that pretty much the same pattern is

154

followed for coal and also natural gas as businesses. Further over and up to the right you'll see that there are three curves which represent profits. In fact, they'd better be higher up on the money scale than the money invested in R&D or the oil company will not have reaped any return on investment for its R&D. The interesting thing to note is that the curves for profit are such that they not only overlap, but they overlap in such a way that for about a thirty-year period the oil company made a pretty steady, high-level rate of return on its investment. In fact, thirty years is so long a time that most people in the company saw this as a natural state of affairs. It goes back to one of our earlier discussions on the failure of success, that is, a very particularized set of conditions for a rather special set of businesses was taken to be something that would hold forever. You'll notice that at the end of the thirty-year cycle there are strong signs, that some people in the company are picking up, that all of these businesses are going to peak. What do you do then? How do you, in other words, cause a very successful dinosaur to change?

Now take a look at Figure 2. What came out during the talk is that there was an underlying fit between the organizational structure of the oil company and the structure of the businesses of its consumers. Figure 2 shows that each of the fossil fuel materials was organized as a separate business within the oil company. Thus, oil was a

THE OIL COMPANY

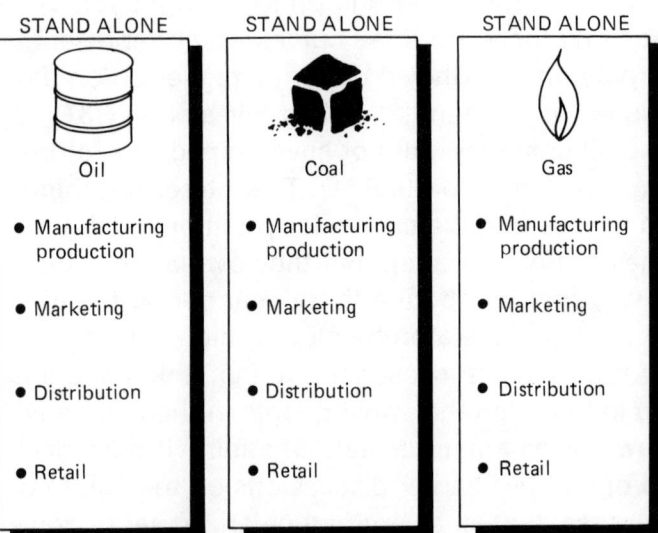

FIGURE 2. The Old Business

separate stand-alone business, coal production was a separate stand-alone, and so was natural gas. Each of these, in effect, had its own vertical company, so they had manufacturing, production, marketing, distribution, and retailing all within them.

Now take a look at Figure 3. What's interesting is that this partitioning of separate stand-alone businesses into autonomous businesses matched almost perfectly the design of buildings up to relatively recent times. That is, buildings had a furnace which used *either* oil *or* coal *or* gas *or*

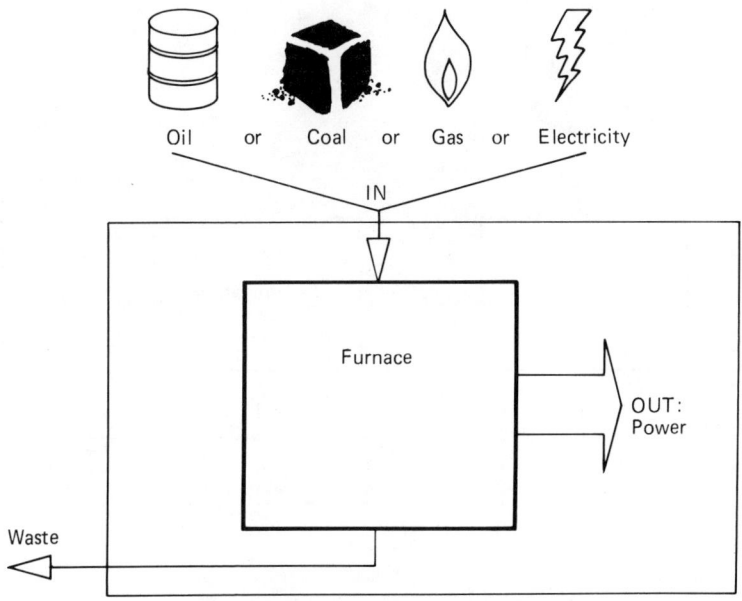

FIGURE 3. The Old Building

electricity, so that the owner of a building had
a choice as to which kind of energy source to
draw upon. Notice also that if you put one of
these materials into your furnace, you got some
power out, and you got some waste that you had
to dispose of since you couldn't really use it.
Again, the point is that the design of old buildings matched the structure of the oil company almost perfectly, that is, you used *one* of the fuels
in your building.

Now take a look at Figure 4. What's amazing
is that because of the development of technol-

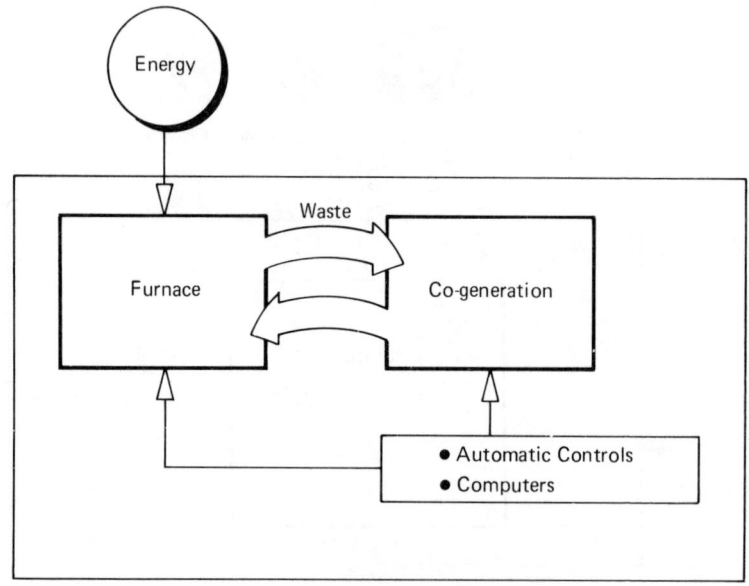

FIGURE 4. The New Building

ogy largely outside of the oil business, buildings began to be redesigned. Figure 4 shows this. It shows that furnaces have become so sophisticated that they are now capable of burning or consuming a variety or a blend of fuels simultaneously. It's no longer a matter of oil *versus* coal *or* gas *or* electricity, but rather what's the proper blend to burn in what combination to get the maximum efficient energy use out of your building.

Look what else is in the diagram. Buildings now have cogeneration devices within them that allow them to burn a variety of input materials more efficiently. Indeed, often the waste from one energy consumption process becomes the input into another kind of furnace or energy device. Also notice that all of this is made possible through the development of automatic controls and computers which allow buildings to monitor their total environment and thus change their energy needs during a total twenty-four-hour cycle. What this means, though, is that the old social contract between the oil company and their consumers has broken down. In the past, the oil company could depend upon the fact that their consumers' buildings were set up to match almost exactly the structure of the company.

This shift is represented by Figure 5. What it says is that the new businesses in the energy field will have to be integrated energy companies which cut across the old stand-alone businesses.

Let me give you the clinker that the speaker presented during his talk. The figures that I've been taking you through are roughly what he presents not only to audiences outside of the industry but also to internal audiences at the oil company where he works. The typical reaction of most people who ascribe to the old conception of the company and the building is the following question: "What are the implications of all these figures for my coal, or my oil, or my gas business?" That's an *appropriate* question from within the old paradigm (Figure 2), but it's an

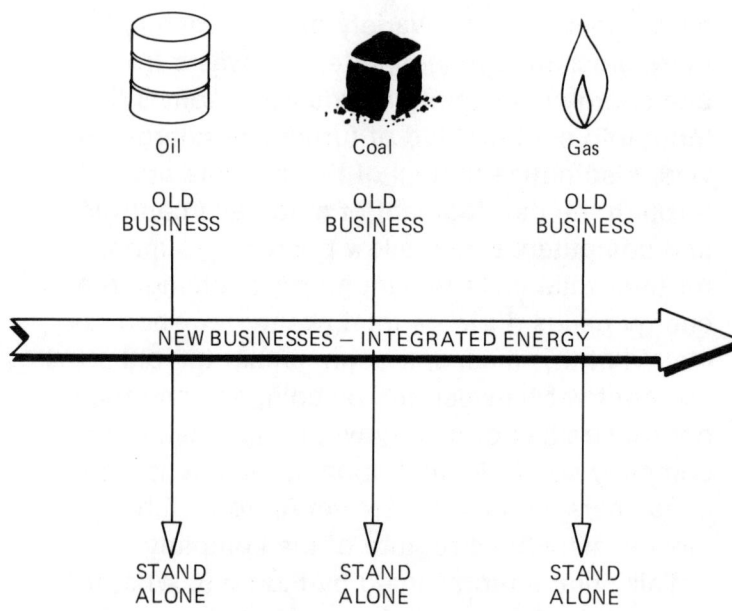

FIGURE 5.   Paradigm Shift

entirely *in*appropriate question from within the new paradigm (Figure 5). But then it's only natural that people would ask a question from an old paradigm if that's the view of the world within which they've been reared and rewarded.

For me, this story isn't just a story of an oil company. It's a story of all businesses, because all we have to do throughout all these figures is take out the words "oil," "coal," "gas," and "electricity" and substitute any other products; these figures apply to any and all businesses. Thus the story is one of a general paradigm switch that is going on in the world today. I don't think we could have a better example of what the old machine view of the world was like, namely one of separate stand-alone businesses as independent cogs in a machine.

The paradigm shift we've been talking about is where everything not only affects everything else but is part of an integrated business. I think the 64-billion-dollar question is what will it take for businesses and managers and executives everywhere not only to appreciate that there is a great paradigm shift going on in the world today, but to stop fighting it and just get on with it. But then, as we both know, that's far too rational a view of how people learn and change. How much more pain will it take, how many more dinosaurs will have to go to the brink of extinction before we get the message that we're facing one of the greatest challenges we've ever faced?

The Stock Market Crash of '87, or We're Running 21st Century Systems with 19th Century Thinking

TO: Steve

FROM: Bob

DATE: August 1, 1989

SUBJECT: The Stock Market Crash of '87, or
         We're Running 21st Century Systems
         with 19th Century Thinking

I've been reflecting on the stock market crash of
'87 and its lessons. I don't want to get caught
up in details, because that is being done by a
host of scholars and presidential commissions.
Instead, I want to emphasize some points that
either have been neglected altogether or have
not been emphasized enough. The first point is
reflected by the title of my memo: We're running
21st century systems with 19th century thinking.
   We humans have incredible will and the ability to bring together the political, economic, and
intellectual resources necessary to create vast,
complex technological systems capable of affecting the entire economy, if not the globe. However, we do not have the will and ability to put together the managerial systems that are necessary
to control this technology. We don't even seem
to be able to pick up the early warning signals,
as one should do in crisis management, to regis-
ter when this technology seems about to get us
into trouble. The point is not just that crises, but

increasingly, megacrises are built into the very fabric of our whole society. The ante keeps going up for crises of all kinds and magnitudes. Indeed, this very fact has created a new kind of crisis. The constant parade of crises confronting us has seemed to anesthetize our very sensitivity to them. Thus, for instance, *The Wall Street Journal,* in a retrospective series of articles on the crash, reported

> How does one separate illusion from reality in an electronic society that serves up visions of disaster nearly every day? It could be that most Americans experienced the crash as yet another media event, something witnessed but not quite real. "People are getting used to the idea of sudden media traumas followed by sudden media recoveries," says Todd Domke, a Boston-area political consultant. "Great public crises come and go—Gary Hart, the Persian Gulf, airplane crashes—but life goes on. People are accepting this weird way of life as a given." (Dennis Farney, "Different Worlds: Main Street's View of The Crash Is Far Different from Wall Street's," *The Wall Street Journal,* Wednesday, December 30, 1987, p. 10. Reprintd by permission of *The Wall Street Journal,* © 1987 Dow Jones and Company, Inc. 1987. All rights reserved.)

To be sure, the signals for a stock market crash were there as early as a year before it occurred. For instance, the November 10, 1986, issue of *Time* magazine reported that the danger signals were evident for the impending crisis, but people wished to either discount them or not take them into account in the first place. For example, *Time* reported that from January 1986 to April 1986 the Dow went from 1502 to 1856, the biggest three-month gain in its history.

Then the market suddenly went into fibrillation. The Dow dropped a bearish 46 points one day (June 9th) and 62 another (July 7th). The bulls came back with a rush on September 4th, when the Dow reached a new all-time high of 1920. But on September 11th and 12th, in a frenzied wave of selling, the Dow slid 121 points, including a one-day drop of 87, the worst ever. Since then, the indicator has continued to jounce at unpredictable intervals in 20- and 30-point jumps and dips, closing last week at 1878, the same level that it had reached in May.

The result of all that unpredictability has been a bull market in benchmarks. No fewer than seven of the ten worst one-day declines in stock-market history, measured in terms of drops in the Dow, have taken place in the past ten months. So have five of the ten best single-day tallies ever recorded. (George Russell, et al., "Manic Market, Is Computer-Driven Stock Trading Good for America?" *Time,* November 10, 1986, pp. 64–65. Copyright 1986 Time Inc. All rights reserved. Reprinted by permission from *Time.*)

So the signals were certainly there, and strong ones they were, that something entirely new was occurring in the stock market. Not only was the market more complex that ever before, but the conditions under which it was operating seemed to be changing as well. For one thing, substantially greater volumes of shares traded on all exchanges. Midwest Stock Exchange Chairman

John Weithers noted, for example, that in the past year his exchange handled more volume than it had in the past 92 years combined! The basic change seems to be that the stock market is no longer driven by a series of small transactions by large numbers of small, single investors; rather, institutional investors who manage large mutual and pension funds are playing an increasingly bigger role. Although it's hard to measure their financial power precisely, especially after the devaluation of securities caused by the crash, a rough estimate is that the big institutional investors control something near a thousand billion dollars. Even though this figure may represent only about a third of the entire equity on U.S. exchanges, these investors make roughly eight out of every ten stock trades on the market each day. Because of their influence and the fact that more and more of their transactions are computerized and occur in big blocks, they send hundreds of millions of dollars cascading in and out of the markets at lightning speed.

In addition, new financial instruments such as index futures have been created which allow the market to function almost as a gigantic casino. Indeed, one wit has noted that even Las Vegas closes down at 5:00 A.M., whereas the stock market is on for gambling 24 hours a day. A recent *Wall Street Journal* article started out by referring to the market as the "Big Casino."

To get an idea of just how pronounced the effects of 21st century technology and systems are, consider this: The big institutional houses have computer programs that automatically trigger huge volumes of trade in and out of the market based on the rise and fall of certain indices. They require six miles of fiber optic and coaxial cables running from securities industry computers to computers at the major brokerage houses, as well as between thousands of personal computers and desktop terminals in the brokerage houses and at least 500 display terminals on the floor of the New York Stock Exchange alone. All of this is necessary to accommodate the huge volume of trade. These computers communicate in a multitude of computer languages and can manage up to a thousand orders a second and a trading volume of 450 million shares daily. The irony is that even this enormous capability wasn't enough, for during the height of the crash it was communications between the exchange and the big investors that broke down, not that between the market and the small investors.

An even greater irony is that no one saw fit to investigate before the crash whether we needed entirely new kinds of managerial systems to control this technology. More energy went into the creation of financial instruments that would take advantage of the market than into designing control systems that would allow us to manage it.

None of this is new; we live in a schizophrenic world. We still function according to the myth that our system is essentially made up of individual investors, when at best we know we have a two-headed system. The truth is that we have created a system of powerful institutional investors who have access to complex trading programs that can take advantage of the differences between the current values of a select group of stocks (for example, the Standard and Poors 500) and new instruments known as *futures indices.* In other words, big investors can supposedly protect their investments by placing "bets," as it were, regarding what they think the values of stocks will be in the future. These investments are open only to large institutional investors, not to small players. Thus considerable creativity and imagination have gone into the creation of new kinds of financial instruments that are tied to computers that small player investors cannot use. Small investors are prevented from using these instruments except by investing in mutual funds that have access to them.

Opponents of greater regulation of the market (e.g., setting up a superagency to manage it more effectively) have a valid point to make, although they don't quite put it in proper perspective. They are right in opposing new control mechanisms in the sense that if a superagency to manage all of these markets were merely another traditional, bureaucratic, governmental agency, it wouldn't work in today's world. Almost by definition, a traditional agency would be strangled by the power and speed of the new technology. The point is that we already know that traditional bureaucratic institutions are no longer sufficient to manage the complexity of a 21st-century technological system. That's why everything is breaking down around us. That's why we produce more and more crises. What the opponents can't seem to realize, however, perhaps because they are cynical about the possibility of getting the necessary legislation through Congress, is that we require entirely new types of institutions to manage in this kind of world.

Perhaps they are right. Perhaps government and the people at large have neither the imagination nor the understanding to design and implement new managerial control systems. Even if we could design them, where would we find enough people to put them into existence? And so we are confronted with paradox again and again. We find imagination, sophistication, and creativity in talented individuals who have been lured away from some of the nation's leading business schools to create entirely new financial instruments in the employ of the large financial brokerage houses. These houses have the ability to put these instruments into being and bring about a new economic system. On the other hand, we do not have the degree of imagination required to hire away some of the country's leading management and political thinkers to help design and create new institutions that would help us *man-*

age the economic mess we've created. We almost seem to have become a society of creating megacrises by design.

To show you how profound the problem is, an article in *Fortune* noted that even if all of these new financial instruments were eliminated altogether from the U.S., "regulatory meddling could drive futures markets offshore." (February 1, 1988, p. 3). This both hits the point exactly on its head and misses it profoundly at the same time. The article is right in the sense that if the U.S. alone prohibits adoption and utilization of the new technologies and the new financial instruments that go hand in hand with them, there is such a demand for them to exploit gaps in the international financial system that somebody somewhere else in the world is more than likely to adopt them. But this argument misses the point in the sense that not only is there only one financial market in the U.S. today because all financial markets are coupled together, but there is also only one financial market in the entire world; it is global. There are no longer separate stock markets, only separate exchanges that are operating 24 hours a day.

Thus, the problem of regulation and control is no longer merely the problem of one country; it is a problem for the system as a whole. The fundamental point is that no control system can work if it is addressed to a level of complexity below that of the thing it is supposed to control. It's like putting in a brain the size of a pea to control something the size of a dinosaur. It just doesn't work for long-term evolution.

The trouble is that this global market is uncoordinated. Perhaps it never can be coordinated, not because of technology alone, but because of the different political purposes of governments. All of which leads us to the purpose of our stock market. Is it primarily a casino operation which people with the cleverest technology can exploit for their own personal gain or the financial gain of the institutions they represent? Or is the primary purpose of the new financial instruments and technology really to enhance the wealth-generating capacity of the economy as a whole? While in the U.S. we are very good at making money for individuals, we're now playing against countries such as Japan and Germany, which are willing to defer profits in the short term for the greater purpose of expanding and generating wealth for their economies as a whole. What we need are control mechanisms for managing a complex system that is not just technical but a combination of complex social, political, and technical forces all at once.

Does mankind have the capability to learn how to think systemically in a world that is now coupled along every one of its dimensions? Does it want to learn? Or is the human capacity for

delusion so great that it will do us in? After all,
barely 11 months before the October stock market crash, *Time* magazine stated,

> The stock market may be faster, rougher and more
> complicated than ever before, but for all its painful
> perils and uncertainties, it is still the best game
> of its kind in town. (George Russell, et al., "Manic
> Market, Is Computer-Driven Stock Trading Good for
> America?" *Time,* November 10, 1986, p. 70. Copyright
> 1986 Time Inc. All rights reserved. Reprinted by
> permission from *Time.*)

What unmitigated chutzpah and gall!

A closing thought:

We've created very clever financial instruments
designed to exploit the differences between the
value of a select group of stocks and indices
that are based on what we think will be the future values of those stocks. These indices were
supposed to lead to safeguards for the investors
in these stocks so that they could not only safe-
guard their investments but actually exploit the
differences between the current values of stocks
and future indices. The trouble is that all of these
so-called safeguards have a strange way of turn-
ing into "more is less." Again, we don't seem to
learn the fundamental point: When you have a
system composed of computer programs designed by huge institutional investors to make decisions on their behalf, and when each program
is largely independent of the others and does not

take into account the actions of the others, the end result can be a situation that is of benefit to no one. Each of the programs takes into account the actions of the others only indirectly at best. In effect, this means that each is in the position of *affecting* the whole system but not of *controlling* it. Each is dependent upon the actions of all the others, and yet each can affect the system in very strong ways. Because no one fully understands these interactions, no one can say that the effect will greatly benefit the economic system rather than lead it to a loss.

For all these reasons, I have to laugh at those who say that greed, not computerized programs, was at the heart of the crash. Of course greed played a fundamental, if not major, role. And yes, of course, no one will ever legislate greed out of existence. But again, this view is too narrow and misses the point. Greed will always operate in human affairs, but no one says it has to operate at lightning speed and be magnified by the latest technology. We may not be able to legislate greed out of existence, but surely we humans have the obligation to examine and limit, if need be, its unrestricted operation through the latest technology.

Epilogue

From the Machine Age to the Systems Age

I

As a civilization, we sit completely astride the machine age and the systems age. As a result, our consciousness, our philosophy, is split right down the middle. One part of our collective mind knows, through the daily bombardment of technology and the advertisements that accompany the technology (witness, for instance, the countless ads on TV and in magazines showing little electrons scurrying everywhere as part of the extended networks that comprise the new telecommunications technologies), that the Systems Age is here beyond any doubt. Thus, while parts of our psyche understand clearly that we are squarely in the Systems Age, other parts do not. Indeed, we resist the idea. In effect, we keep on trying to solve the problems of the Systems Age with our old Machine Age mentality.

Some of this is due to just plain old-fashioned denial. It is part of the difficulty involved in making the transition that any profound revolution in human affairs calls for. Even more fundamental is the fact that we have not disseminated widely the new tools that would allow people to think systemically even if they wanted to.

One of the important lessons of this book is that there *are* tools available for thinking systemically. Indeed, they form an essential part of a whole new way of thinking. A critical component of this new thinking is a far deeper appreciation of paradox and the absolutely vital role that assumptions play in treating all problems.

From this perspective, *all* problems, no matter how different on the surface from one another, are the same beneath. Also, all problems are interconnected, so they can no longer be solved in isolation from one another. For example, employees can no longer be viewed as mere cogs in some gigantic machine. If an employee fails or doesn't work out, another cannot merely be plopped down in his or her place without harmful effects to the personnel system of the entire organization.

Assumptions are like the weather; everyone acknowledges their critical importance, but no one does anything about them. No one offers a systematic way of getting at them and of assessing their relative impact.

The systematic assessment of assumptions has been one of the primary aims of this book. The argument is that the task has become too critical to be left to chance. It must become part and parcel of the everyday thinking and behavior of all organizations that wish to survive. Through the interchange of memos between two CEOs, we have had the opportunity not only to see how a method for getting at assumptions surfaces in the discussions between them, but also to witness how it is directly applicable to their ongoing problems.

II

A word needs to be said about the nature of the two CEOs and what they stand for. The sensitive reader will notice that the dialogue between them occurs mainly on an intellectual plane. This is not to say that pain and emotions do not intrude explicitly into their conversations. They do. Still, we know little of the extended personal and emotional lives of the characters.

It should be clear that their personal and emotional lives are important. We know from recent studies that working in any large-scale, modern institution takes a heavy toll on its participants. Recent studies show all too clearly the price we pay for success in our society.

It should also be clear, even from the limited conversation that takes place on the emotional level, not only that there is no significant change without considerable pain, but that unless the pain is dealt with directly, either through counseling or therapy, there really is no hope of significant change either within individuals or their organizations. We kid ourselves when we think that our problems can be dealt with purely at the intellectual level. The memos in this book, as limited as they are in digging deep down into the emotional lives of the characters, show nonetheless that an emotional transformation, not

181

just an intellectual one, takes place within and between them. Unless one is prepared to face directly the pain with which all human beings must deal, and deal with it in serious ways, there won't be much change.

Yet for all this acknowledgment, we still don't really get to know the characters. This was done explicitly because the executives who could write the memos in this book are rare. In our society, at least, it is unusual for men to open up deeply to one another either intellectually or emotionally.

I should make it clear that even on a purely intellectual level, the number of executives who could articulate, let alone appreciate, all the arguments contained in this book is small. However, for this reason, it is even more important to emphasize that I have met those special few who have been more than able to do it. The memos contained in this book are not purely fictitious creations. The most able executives I've encountered have articulated most if not all of the arguments and are certainly able to appreciate them. However, I would be dishonest if I contended that the exchanges between the two CEOs are the norm. They are not. It's precisely for this reason that a proper subtitle for *Break-Away Thinking* would have been "Memos That Top Executives *Should* Write to One Another," not "Memos That They *Are* Writing to One Another."

I have no doubt whatsoever that if our society is to make the transition successfully to the Systems Age and thereby continue to be a major player in the global economy, then more and more executives will have to learn to expand their thinking. One cannot grapple with the problems of the Systems Age with Machine Age thinking.

Richard J. Barnet, writing in the *The New Yorker*, has stated the matter extremely well. We would all be well advised not only to take his thoughts seriously but to internalize them:

> The strength of the nation now depends more and more upon economic health and political resilience. It cannot be calculated by counting weapons or by keeping books on the small victories and setbacks that are the lot of a great power in a world too dangerous for war. The very way national security is defined creates problems, for it is almost always defined in military terms, and the *assumption* [my emphasis] usually is that there is some military answer. But for great powers with much to lose, democracies especially, victories are becoming increasingly elusive. More than ever, the strength of a nation rests on the morale of its people, on their capacity for innovating, for producing, and for adapting to the new circumstances. The influence of the United States on the world will depend less on the state of the nuclear stockpile and more on the strength of the commitment to regenerate American society and to help build a more secure and peaceful world. *Security is achieved not by posturing but by understanding the real forces at work in the world and taking intelligent action in respect to them* [my empha-

sis]. (Richard J. Barnet, "Reflections, the Four Pillars." Reprinted by permission; © 1987 Richard J. Barnet. Originally in *The New Yorker,* March 9, 1987, p. 89.)

III

Neither the values of a society nor its detailed policies are really independent of the larger collective social fabric which holds it together. If this is indeed the case, then we have come full circle to where this book began. If it requires pain for individuals to change, and even craziness to break with old patterns, as the very first memos in this book attest, then what kind of pain and craziness will it take to change the values of our society so that we can be more fully competitive in today's world?

Even if we cannot answer such questions at the present, we can at least begin to feel, however vaguely, that a new story or myth is beginning to take shape that can serve as a collective vision to guide our society through the revolution we are experiencing. Like all myths, it begins with a very dim stirring; we can only perceive its rough outlines; thus, we're in no position to specify what it will look like in final detail. However, one thing is clear; its very centerpiece is built upon a declaration of interdependency. It's no longer viable to form the basis of any nation on the notion of an "us" versus a "them." There is no more "us versus them." By now, surely one of the most famous punch lines of cartoonist Walt Kelly's Pogo is familiar to everyone. It has been quoted one too many times, but it is still true: "We have met the enemy and he is us." Bhopal and Chernobyl have put to rest for all time the dangerous illusion of an "us" versus a "them" in a world that has now shrunk more than any of us could ever have imagined.

Part of this new but barely discernible myth are such elements as the belief that government can no longer be regarded as an enemy. If it is not an ally and certainly not benevolent in all societies, a fact no one would contest or doubt, then the challenge is to design governments and institutions that are congruent with an interdependent world.

By the same token, the collective teamwork that our society needs to fashion new solutions does not mean a mindless groupism. For the question is not whether America and any other society needs lone men and women of genius; it always has and always will. The point is how they can combine their talents to produce the solutions that the world now requires.

In sum, our vision needs to be as broad as the entity we are now capable of affecting, that is, the entire globe, if not the solar system and beyond. The late E. F. Schumacher, author of *Small Is Beautiful*, said it best: "Man is so clever a species, he will not survive without wisdom." In sum, the wisdom we now need is global, a wisdom matched to the size of the challenges we face.

185

Notes

Memos 1 and 2 are based on:

David A. Garvin, "Quality Problems, Policies, and Attitudes in the United States and Japan: An Exploratory Study," *Academy of Management Journal,* 29(4), December 1986, 653–673.

J. C. Abegglen, and G. Stalk, Jr., *Kaisha, the Japanese Corporation.* New York: Basic Books, 1985.

James R. Lincoln, Mitsuyo Hanada, and Kerry McBride, "Organizational Structures in Japanese and U.S. Manufacturing," *Administrative Science Quarterly,* 31(3), September 1986, 338–364.

Memos 3 and 4 are based on:

Leon F. Seltzer, *Paradoxical Strategies in Psychotherapy: A Comprehensive Overview and Guidebook.* New York: Wiley, 1986.

Kenwyn K. Smith, and David N. Berg, *Paradoxes of Group Life: Understanding Conflict, Paralysis, and Movement in Group Dynamics.* San Francisco: Jossey-Bass, 1987.

Memos 5 and 6 are based primarily on:

Russell L. Ackoff, *Creating the Corporate Future: Plan or Be Planned For.* New York: Wiley, 1981.

M. J. Piore, and C. F. Sabel, *The Second Industrial Divide.* New York: Basic Books, 1984.

Robert B. Reich, *The Next American Frontier.* New York: Times Books, 1983.

Robert B. Reich, *Tales of a New America.* New York: Times Books, 1987.

Lester Thurow, *The Zero-Sum Solution: Building a World-*

Class American Economy. New York: Simon & Schuster, 1985.

The *Washington Post* article referred to is by Sharon Walsh, "U.S. Travel Industry Has 'Worst Year' Ever," *Washington Post,* Sunday, December 28, 1986, pp. K1–K2.

The following also played a key role in this section:

J.C. Abegglen, and G. Stalk, Jr., *Kaisha, the Japanese Corporation.* New York: Basic Books, 1985.

W. J. Abernathy, and others, *Industrial Renaissance: Producing a Competitive Future for America.* New York: Basic Books, 1983.

B. Bluestone, and B. Harrison, *The Deindustrialization of America.* New York: Basic Books, 1982.

James Fallows, "America's Changing Economic Landscape," *Atlantic,* March, 1985, p. 56.

Donald Gervirtz, *Business Plan for America: An Entrepreneur's Manifesto.* New York: Putnam, 1984.

I.C. Magaziner, and Robert B. Reich, *Minding America's Business: The Decline and Rise of the American Economy.* New York: Vintage, 1983.

Ian I. Mitroff, *Business Not As Usual: Rethinking Our Individual, Corporate, and Industrial Strategies for Global Competition.* San Francisco: Jossey-Bass, 1987.

Ian I. Mitroff, and Ralph H. Kilmann, *Corporate Tragedies: Product Tampering, Sabotage, and Other Catastrophes.* New York: Praeger, 1984.

Kevin Phillips, *Staying on Top: The Business Case for a National Industrial Strategy.* New York: Random House, 1984.

Paul Shrivastava, *Bhopal: Anatomy of a Disaster.* New York: Harper & Row, 1987.

Memo 7. The tables for Memo 7 are drawn from:

Ian I. Mitroff, *Business Not As Usual; Rethinking Our Individual, Corporate, and Industrial Strategies for Global Competition.* San Francisco: Jossey-Bass, 1987.

See also the following:

W. J. Abernathy, and others, *Industrial Renaissance: Producing a Competitive Future for America.* New York: Basic Books, 1983.

Paul R. Lawrence, and D. Dyer, *Renewing American Industry.* New York: The Free Press, 1983.

Brock Yates, *The Decline and Fall of the American Automobile Industry.* New York: Vintage Books, 1984.

The discussion of General Motors in particular is drawn from the following paper:

James O'Toole, "Declining Innovation: The Failure of Success, a Summary Report of the Seventh Twenty Year Forecast Project." Center for Futures Research, Graduate School of Business, University of Southern California, 1983, pp. 1–28.

Memos 8 and 9. Readers interested in pursuing the whole subject of how to surface and critique assumptions further and more systematically should consult the following:

Russell L. Ackoff, *Creating the Corporate Future: Plan or Be Planned For.* New York: Wiley, 1981.

Ralph H. Kilmann, *Beyond the Quick-Fix: Managing Five*

Tracks to Organizational Success. San Francisco: Jossey-Bass, 1984.

Harold Linstone, *The Multiperspective Method.* Reading, MA: Addison-Wesley, 1984.

Richard O. Mason, and Ian I. Mitroff, *Challenging Strategic Planning Assumptions.* New York: Wiley, 1981.

Ian I. Mitroff, and Ralph H. Kilmann, *Corporate Tragedies, Product Tampering, Sabotage, and Other Catastrophes.* New York: Praeger, 1984.

Ian I. Mitroff, Richard O. Mason, and Vincent P. Barabba, *The 1980 Census: Policy Making Amid Turbulence.* Lexington, MA: Lexington Books, 1983.

Ian I. Mitroff, *Business Not As Usual: Rethinking Our Individual, Corporate, and Industrial Strategies for Global Competition.* San Francisco: Jossey-Bass, 1987.

Finally, for a discussion on the subjectivity of physical science, not just social science, see:

Ian I. Mitroff, *The Subjective Side of Science: A Philosophical Inquiry into the Psychology of the Apollo Moon Scientists.* Amsterdam: Elsevier, 1974.

Memos 10, 11, 12, and 13: For an introduction to some of the literature on crisis management, see the following:

Stephen Fink, *Crisis Management.* New York: AMACOM, 1986.

Ian I. Mitroff, and Ralph H. Kilmann, *Corporate Tragedies, Product Tampering, Sabotage, and Other Catastrophes.* New York: Praeger, 1984.

Ian I. Mitroff, Terry C. Pauchant, and Paul Shrivastava, "The Structure of Man-Made Organizational Crises:

Conceptual and Empirical Issues in the Development of a General Theory of Crisis Management." (Graduate School of Business, Center For Crisis Management, University of Southern California, Los Angeles, CA 90089-1421, paper submitted for publication), 1987.

Ian I. Mitroff, Terry C. Pauchant, and Paul Shrivastava, "Forming a Crisis Portfolio: Putting One's Crisis Preparations on a Firmer Footing." (Graduate School of Business, Center For Crisis Management, University of Southern California, Los Angeles, CA 90089-1421, paper submitted for publication, 1987.

Paul Shrivastava, *Bhopal: Anatomy of a Crisis,* Cambridge, MA: Ballinger, 1987.

Report of the President's Commission on the Space Shuttle Challenger Accident. (Order No. 04000000496-3). Washington, DC: Government Printing Office.

Memos 14 and 15:

J. C. Abegglen, and G. Stalk, Jr., *Kaisha, the Japanese Corporation.* New York: Basic Books, 1985.

Russell L. Ackoff, *Creating the Corporate Future: Plan or Be Planned For.* New York: Wiley, 1981.

Robert Jervis, *The Illogic of American Nuclear Strategy.* New York: Cornell, 1984.

Ian I. Mitroff, "The Complete and Utter Failure of Traditional Thinking in Comprehending the Nuclear Dilemma: Why It's Impossible to Formulate a Paradox-Free Theory of Nuclear Strategy," *Journal of Technological Forecasting and Social Change,* 1986, 29, 51–72.

C. A. Zraket, "Uncertainties in Building a Strategic Defense," *Science, 235,* March 27, 1987, 1600–1606.

Memos 16 and 17:

Robert N. Bellah, and others, *Habits of the Heart: Individualism and Commitment in American Life.* Berkeley, CA: University of California Press, 1985.

Tami R. Davis, and Sean M. Lynn-Jones, "City Upon a Hill," *Foreign Policy, 66,* Spring 1987, 20–38.

Neil Postman, *Amusing Ourselves to Death: Public Discourse in the Age of Show Business.* New York: Viking, 1985.

Richard Schickel, *Intimate Strangers: The Culture of Celebrity.* New York: Doubleday, 1985.

Epilogue. For the price we pay for success, see:

Douglas La Bier, *Modern Madness: The Emotional Fallout of Success.* Menlo Park, CA: Addison-Wesley, 1986.

Index